GATHERED:
CONTEMPORARY QUAKER POETS

COPYRIGHT © 2013
ISBN: 978-1-939675-01-9
PUBLISHED BY SUNDRESS PUBLICATIONS

EDITOR: NICK MCRAE
NICK@SUNDRESSPUBLICATIONS.COM
HTTP://WWW.SUNDRESSPUBLICATIONS.COM

COLOPHON: THIS BOOK IS SET IN BASKERVILLE.

COVER IMAGE: RON WADDAMS

COVER DESIGN: RHONDA LOTT

BOOK DESIGN: ERIN ELIZABETH SMITH & NICK MCRAE

GATHERED:
CONTEMPORARY QUAKER POETS

EDITED BY ~~NICK McRAE~~

To Kimberly,

for keeping me alive and
content on the Never-Ending
Trail of Doom, and for
being radiant all the while.

—Nick

1/29/14 Jupiter House,
Denton, TX

CONTENTS

EDITOR'S NOTE

Gathered here in this volume are poems by men and women from all over the United States and abroad whose lives have been in some way formed by the spiritual community that is the Religious Society of Friends, known as Quakers. There are liberal Quakers and conservative Quakers. There are Quakers from all points on the cultural and religious spectrum. There are lifelong Quakers, Quakers from hybrid spiritual backgrounds, and those who were once part of Quaker society but have since moved on down other paths. Though all of these poets have been touched by the Quaker way of life, the work presented here is not religious or devotional in the traditional sense. Many poems address Quaker culture and spirituality, but they question those traditions, taking a broader view of the human condition and the experience of living in our complex, often troubling world, where there are no easy answers.

This anthology takes its title—*Gathered*—from the Quaker concept of the "gathered meeting." Thomas Kelly (1893–1941), influential Quaker thinker and mystic, describes his understanding of the gathering experience (in the appropriately titled essay "The Gathered Meeting") like this:

> In the Quaker practice of group worship on the basis of silence come special times when an electric hush and solemnity and depth of power steals over the worshippers. A blanket of divine covering comes over the room, and a quickening Presence pervades us, breaking down some part of the special privacy and

isolation of our individual lives and bonding our spirits within a super-individual Life and Power—an objective, dynamic Presence which enfolds us all, nourishes our souls, speaks glad, unutterable comfort within us, and quickens in us depths that had before been slumbering. The Burning Bush has been kindled in our midst, and we stand together on holy ground.

I was a poet before I became a Quaker, and when as a new member I first ran across the passage from Kelly, I was struck by how aptly it described the thing I loved most about poetry: that sense of being enfolded in and nourished by it, of being forced out of myself and bonded to something—a word, a tradition, a community—that was more and greater and more meaningful than my own subjectivity. It is my hope that the poems collected here will become, in their gatheredness, more than the sum of their parts, beautiful though those parts may already be.

I would like to extend heartfelt gratitude to the many people who supported me during the past few years and helped make this book possible. I thank Erin Elizabeth Smith, T.A. Noonan, Rhonda Lott, Meagan Cass, Beth Couture, and the rest of the Sundress Publications family for their invaluable assistance and for welcoming me into the fold with this collection. I thank the Quaker community I found in the Carrollton Friends Worship Group and North Columbus Friends Meeting for shining Light so brightly on me, and I thank all of the contributors gathered here for shining theirs on all of us. I thank my teachers— Chad Davidson, Greg Fraser, Andrew Hudgins, Kathy Fagan, Henri Cole, Michelle Herman, Emily Hipchen, Thomas Lux, Mark Jarman, Daniel Anderson, Claudia

Emerson, Wyatt Prunty, Sidney Wade, Dave Smith, G.C. Waldrep, Branda Hillman, and many others—for showing me better ways to love the written word. I thank my dearest comrade poets, especially Eric Smith, Alex Fabrizio, Matt Sumpter, Emilia Phillips, and Analicia Sotelo, for their boundless love and patience. I thank Katharine Johnsen for being the best part of every single day. I thank my family for always believing in me. And I thank you, dear readers, for believing in poetry enough to buy or borrow this book. This is all for you.

Nick McRae

ROSALIE MOFFETT

SUNDAY EVENING MEETING FOR WORSHIP AT 1435 COLUMBIA ST. APT. 2

Wine, spare me. Pare
me—by which I mean make me
Quaker-simple and Quaker-silent. In order

to hear the gnats, the fruit-fly, I sit
in a fermentation—meditation? It's a mix
when I close my eyes, of darkness and swimming

points of white. I am quiet. I lean side to side
the way I have seen praying mantises do.
I clasp my hands, wait for the Light.

Kitchen table, consecrated
edifice, if there is anything holy about this
it's how hard it is
to wait. And the fact that I am still

here. Wine, I credit you. Though who can blame me
if, when I think of Light I ask *electricity?*
Ah, but, Livingston Rosé, the whole idea
is that I am my own

minister. So what if you are all gone, save
a pink ring? I'm here. I can almost hear
the no-see-ums.

ROSALIE MOFFETT

KNECHT W/ NATURE

Sometimes I believe the landscaping
truck full of tree limbs
with the bumper sticker that says "Trees don't bleed"

because I believe in a certain limblessness—
I believe in the painless beauty of that
move toward cordless,
and then cell.

My iPhone is a small room.
It arrived without umbilical cord. Branchless,
doorless. I want this isolation.
I just want a trunk

the size of my grandfather's cigarette tin
to put everything in without the hassle
of lineage. The Airedale wags its cropped tail
anyway, I've noticed. They've made

the garden into a perfect line
of small pruned box-bushes. On every
cut, there are little yellow-sap topazes
like my birthstone earrings.

ROSALIE MOFFETT

INSTAR AND ECLOSE

I know metamorphosis turns
a kaleidoscope

into a caterpillar and then into a gypsy moth
with a furry mouth. I've learned

some things.
To mimic injury

the plover fakes an ineffectual
wing. Failure: the lure

of a wound is always enticing
away from something

smaller, more
vulnerable. Everything

I've ever kissed
was a tree

in boy's clothing. Every time I've yawned
it's tasted like apples. I climb

into the white silk gown—it's more
a question

of revision—made by tent caterpillars.
They ruin the tree into a shimmering.

JENNIFER LUEBBERS

[BECAUSE IT IS PERISHABLE,]

the day, with its vinegar &

orange, its coffee gone
       cold & porridge

solid on the sill, I try to imagine
       a door that opens

to a meadow, where we ride
       in carriages

to castles haloed by moats—
       fold foil

into boats to careen down-
       stream, carve

a carousel of swans with
       wings

that do not sink, that carry us
       over banks

of clover where we stroke
       silver the beards

of goats, where the throats
       of the lilies

8

open for the bees——
          & there is pollen

on our knees——& here,
          friend, the trees

are chandeliers that burn
          the river

with sapphire light, & we sip
          its water

from a teacup's chipped
          lip, & you say what

we really want is someone
          to witness each day:

our names for each other,
          our words for things——

always, friend, I will hear
          your voice

singing in the sound
          of paper.

Exorcism with Ancestors

The women came to cure, though I had no demons.
    They laid their hands on me to heal

though I did not think myself ill. I traced a man's name

in the fogged mirror—it kept coming back,
    so I could believe he would, too. *His words*

be but wind, the women warned, *his promises*

but rain[1]. I did not want their intercessions:
    not the candles they crossed

at my throat, not the water they drew to cool

my wrists. I did not want their hands hovered over
    my head in prayer, not the altar of incense

they built at my feet. But what could I do,

except leave them to their work? What else
    could I do, but stare up at the ceiling, its pattern

of plaster stars? If they could erase the constellations

his mouth made on my body, they could not reverse
    the belt's unlatching—

---

1 Words allegedly spoken by Saint Agatha

how I'd prayed for that sound like a coin in a plate—

a stigmata I'd willed into my outstretched palm.

JENNIFER LUEBBERS

WOMAN IN STARVING TIME

1609–10, Virginia

Then winter settled in our stomachs,
      and when my husband returned

from the woods with an empty sack,
      I sharpened the axe, hacked

the throats of *Dogges* and horses—
      of *Rates* and mice and snakes.

In the first months of marriage, we'd believed
      abundance possible.

Then, enough possible. But it was not,
      and so he blessed

the blade, broke me, consecrated
      me, consumed me. It is

written that *he fedd upon her*
      till he had clean devoured

all her partes, then burned at the stake.
      Another woman lived

through that winter, birthed
      a daughter, named her Virginia.

In this story, the word *slaughter*
        is replaced with the word

survival; my forgotten name
        becomes the flames that leap

from flesh inside flesh. This new
        world, like the old, still loves

the sacrificial body, still
        seeks baptism by fire.

JENNIFER LUEBBERS

DOXOLOGY FOR THE BROTHER

Glory be to the boy who waits till his sister is in the backyard,
      sunning on a towel in her string bikini that sags,

now, at her waist; glory to he who waits till she's coated

her clavicle in tanning oil before he slips into her room, unfolds
      the accordion doors of her closet, and unhooks,

from the padded hanger, the straps of the silver dress she wore

to the spring formal—glory to the boy who likes the way it makes
      his flat chest looks fuller, the way the angle

of the afternoon sun hits the sequins and spangles the walls—

boy who can think of nothing he can say to save
      her, but who, that summer, will eat everything

she will not: ears of corn roasted in their husks, burgers still pink

at the center, cold melon and cookie dough ice cream and Key
      Lime pie; glory to he who will grow too big

for the dress, who will take, then, his sister's tube of mascara,

close his eyes and remember how, when he was still
      very small, he would lie face down in the garden

walled with ripe tomatoes and thick vines—how he thought, then,

that if he couldn't see, no one could see him—but how always
      his sister would find him, and lift him from the fragrant dirt—

and when their mother called, they would part the curtain

of grill smoke, and together, with earth on their hands, go inside
      for supper.

JENNIFER LUEBBERS

PETITIONS

Let us pray for linked arms. For Red Rover Red Rover.
For Luke's headlong lunge into our locked fingers

and the wind we knock from his lungs.

Pray for the parish green, its clipped edges and chemical
quiet. For halls honeycombed in mustard tile

and soured cartons of cafeteria milk. For fish sticks

and Velveeta on Fridays. Let us Sundays to pluck
the spindled legs off spiders. Let us summer's fireflies,

their abdomens to smear on our lips. Let us burn

beneath the sun—and when we turn thirteen and take
the names of virgin saints whose blood poured

to wine, whose suffering became stars—let us

kneel in the little Gethsemanes of our mothers'
gardens, genuflect among hostas and heliotrope,

and pray to escape what's prophesied: how we'll betray

our thighs to the mosquito's bite; how we'll loosen
hold of each others' hands; how we'll let Luke

and the other boys make the break

and the benediction of ticks go to bed in our skin.

BARN ELEGY

The city sends the men to burn.
When we stand on the porch to watch

them douse the tumbled beams
in kerosene, to see the empty silo sink

to soot, you unloose your hand.
You shade your eyes against the flame.

You say, It's best. It's in this town's
best interest, the papers say, the marshal says—

say the men sent to rehearse the rescue.
Now, when I wake, another house

is risen on ash. Again, the scorched world
thirsts. When the new wife calls her husband

out to the yard, to lie against her in the grass,
I dream I hear another woman's voice calling

up from a well. Were this another century,
I would break, each morning, the pail's lip

of ice. Were this another century, you would stay
because there'd be no other place to go.

APPROPRIATED

I cost one howling year, and gods.[1]
    And when Simon saw that through laying
    on of the apostles' hands the Holy Ghost was given,
    he offered them money[2]: $1.3 trillion.[3]

Dear, I never thought I would cost that much.
    Nor would teleology: the price of laying on hands
    across your soft-wet belly, cost of babies
    checkpoints and Faust-black nightmares.

There were my legs, entwined with yours, and there
    congressional appropriations, untwining
    us from the same. Laying on hands....
    the papal forehead struck three times with a hammer.

Every rock of sand holds election. Tal Afar, Iraq: 18 Jan. 2005.
    When the bishops have it right, the smoke burns white.
    Eligo in Summum Pontificem   Samar Hassan
    who elected that night sprouting hair in the moonlight

constellations crackling the sedan's windshield when her parents
    didn't stop at the darkened checkpoint, blood-patterned
    sidewalk where the photographer stalked, missing
    the olive private's weeping. Also Heidi Klum on O'Brien.

---

1   From Canto III
2   Acts 8:18
3   From "Costs of War," the Eisenhower Study Group, Brown University

Mere democracy John Winthrop loathed when he split[+]
the sodomizer's tongue, removed ears, thanked god
for election. Did not see, nor I, the sand mouth swallows
speeding toward the checkpoint.

DAWN POTTER

LULLABY

The lilacs are fading; their petals are falling.
The ants have crawled into their holes.
The children are restlessly tossing their beds.
The horses are chasing their foals.

The dark, oh the dark, flies upon us so fast.
The little boys roll up and down.
Their feet kick the walls, and they churn up the sheets,
while sailors jump ship and then drown,

and armies hunt men, and butchers kill hogs,
and hurricanes level the towns
on the coast where the sea goes on slapping the shore,
and the dogs run careening like clowns.

NOSTALGIA

It was darker then, in the nights when the cars
Came sliding around the traffic circle, when the headlights
Speckled with rain traveled the bedroom walls
and vanished; when the typewriter, the squeaking chair,
the slow voice of the radio stirred the night air like a fan.
Of course, the ones we loved were beautiful—
slim, dark-haired, intent on their books.
The rain came swishing against the lamp-lit windows.
The cat purred in his chair. A clock sang,
and we lay nearly asleep, almost dreaming,
almost alone, nearly gone—the days fly so;
and the nights, like sleep, disappear without memory.

DAWN POTTER

BLUE

Once upon a time there is an hour,
        rainless, starless. And then
a subtle hand unmasks a claw.
        Bone speaks to bone. A cower
roughens a curve; famine gnaws
        at tender flanks, grips bone, again,
again, tearing, shredding, once upon a time
        sleep pretends to fight, once
an hour shivers into dead rain, dry stars;
        into glory, first maculate chime
of defeat—bruise or savor, a barred
        owl's wail, the shrew that it hunts.

Mrs. Dickinson Waits in the Car

My Mother does not care for thought—
   Emily Dickinson

         A few meager stars, a hazy moon
      brighter than old Kentuck,
and a bulge of frost spooned
      across the windshield like a plucked,

         flash-frozen chick. Into this arctic
      chariot, the heater chafes and spouts
its idiot vows. Yes, I lied about Kentuck.
      No doubt, it's glowing like all get-out,

         like a pair of gibbous moons, like molten
      honey dripped into a summer lake.
Blame art, then: I've been soaking up Bolton's
      poems, and now I'm acting like a fake

         southerner, which is to say gothically
      depressed while making love to every rum-
soaked predicate I meet. Treat *gothically*
      as a ringer for New England numb.

         Today a friendly rube lauded my skill
      at prosy contemplation, but what a crock.
Call a heart a spade: call me a fading, moody kill-
      joy with a romance eye for loss and schlock.

The car fan chatters hopelessly; newsmen
chant wind-chill rates and hockey stats.
Like any hausfrau I fret over loaves in the oven,
socks on the line, carboys of milk, and ruinous vats

of soup. There they burn or boil.
Here I dally in this wrapper-strewn capsule,
this (laugh with me!) bell jar. Can I stand loyal
to her, cruel queen of diction, and also rule

my roost, my squat piratical outpost?
I shiver; I prop my tome of poems
against the cruiser's plastic wheel. I boast
that they age for *me:* these jeroboams

of syntax, these sherry cups of rage.
Yet these tired hands; yet these cold feet.
Go ahead: remind me to shut up, to flip the page,
to change the station, to bleat

of Mother's lonely vigil.
I'm not proud of my idle arrogance.
Meanwhile, the rye loaf chars and the milk spills.
They're out of my ken, for a hatful of minutes.

Let me claim to be oracular.
"Poetry is not like reasoning," urges Shelley.
And I reply: "nothing in particular"
is the maiden speech of every tragedy.

DAWN POTTER

PROTESTANT CEMETERY

Here lies one whose name was writ in water.

Keats is dead, time's swift apprentice
tramping the grimy London lanes,
pockets crammed with pencil stubs, two mice,
a half-penned letter of delight—"ah!
had I never known your kindness…"

and Shelley is dead, one white hand
clutching a tinker-toy mast,
silk scarf flying, a torrent of curls
shock-whipped by wind, and the sea
tearing sheets from her bed;

and baby Severn is dead, reckless
philosopher of floors and stairwells,
founder of speech, tyrant-prince,
squawking cricket, famished
at twilight and dawn;

and here they lurk, next door to a squatty
pyramid, ten or twelve feral cats, a flea market
packed with bargain-mad nuns; and before us,
a whistling man digging a ditch. Two pear-shaped
English ladies consult a guidebook,

peering anxiously at a laurel shrub
for aid; the cheerful digger, unconsulted,

26

flaps a dirty hand toward the damp corner
where Keats and baby Severn hide,
not far from baby Shelley,

though Shelley himself is stuffed into denser
congress, cheek-to-jowl with Corso,
that misbegotten seeker, and a thousand other
amputated poets, Christian soldiers, wastrel
lovers of light not cited in the ladies' guidebook

or anywhere else, for that matter,
a collection of forgotten Protestants farmed out
for eternity to this heretic Anglo-Saxon outpost
nestled at the bony knee of an ancient dump,
by far the tidiest park I've seen in Rome.

Compare the Aventine on Sunday morning—
parade of chubby brides and crabby mothers,
grooms dangling like haute-couture chimps
from the orange trees, high-heeled grandmas
shaking fists at pig-headed husbands who refuse

to beam, a dozen stray soccer balls, bums snoring
in the lanky grass, and beyond us, all Rome
painted under the haze like a tacky postcard.
They don't let bums nap in the Protestant Cemetery,
though it would be a pleasant place to rest,

like sleeping in the Secret Garden, high-walled
and remote, a clipped thick lawn, green
as a golf course, smooth footpaths, and neat little
English-speaking arrows directing mourners
to "Gramsci" and "W.C."

It's a relief to us Protestants, this orderly
plantation, yet even here Italian chaos

creeps over the fence: Where is the "Keats" sign?
worry the English ladies, fidgeting at the edge
of the ditch. The digger lays down his spade,

waves both hands toward the corner,
smile packed with intention, but does he intend
"Keats"? The ladies retreat into their sunhats,
nod wanly, then too vigorously, then hasten
precipitously into the shade, pretending to search

for Shelley. Only when my friend and I forge
boldly over the ditch and beeline a placid trio
of stones do the ladies brake and regress, politely
hovering with cameras while I examine the earth
for traces of violets (none) and consider

the fate of baby Severn, dead of an accident,
age one year. Another predestined blunder—
tipped out of a casement, choked on marzipan,
crushed by the cart of a fruit vendor...
My friend, a Sicilian Catholic from New Jersey,

amiably shouts, "Grazie!" at the digger,
who murmurs, "Prego, prego," and eyes her tits.
It's our last day in Rome, and she is humoring me,
killing time with dead poets and babies
when we could be squatting on the hot

Pantheon steps devouring artichokes
and strawberries from a plastic bag.
She flits her false lashes knowingly
at the digger, shifts her brassy red
pocketbook to the other freckled shoulder;

and the fidgeting ladies, alarmed,
are nonetheless impressed by her sang-froid,
another trait of my hungry people—
this laborious, admiring fear of eros:
and it *is* lovely,

the digger's desire, my friend's frank
acknowledgment, though I, like the ladies,
blush and scuttle. Shelley, poor sap,
doing his Jim-Morrison dance all over town,
wasn't, at heart, much better off;

he had to invent a sort of faith transcending
faithlessness—a house of cards
that would have crushed him in the end,
if the gulf hadn't eaten him first. The digger
commences his whistle, my friend and I recede,

the ladies, shy as ducks, open their *Portable
Romantics* and murmur a brief hymn;
the short lady sighs and closes her damp eyes:
all praise, they sing, to Keats,
bright star, alone and palely loitering.

Dying, you came staggering to Rome to live,
choking on black phlegm and gore,
dim eyes fixed on a gaudy sky.
And left behind your tired epitaph.
Nothing we make will matter.

Here it idles, scratched into the mossy
opalescent damp, embroidered with a passel
of lament you didn't want to hear.
But too little is never enough for our people,
once we've been jolted to love;

and I know baby Severn's father loved you,
dragging his nursemaid bones
down to the city limits sixty years later,
waiting out Judgment Day with you
and his child in arms, under the noon

jangle of a dozen Holy Roman church bells,
trams hissing to a stop, digger whistling an unknown
tune, my friend crossing herself, tendering
a muttered prayer for her cancer-mangled breast.
I'd light a candle, my brothers, if that were our way.

A LETTER TO MY ADVISOR IN ZOOLOGY

Gabe,
The honey comb
drips its juice on you, but
you ain't sweet.

How can I tell you
about mountains
when you want your feet
in the mud
the low ground
     low down
         earth.

With you, it was crystal towers
showers of DNA letters
and jargon
and worn out words.
Over and over and over and over
and   I needed you
     no more

No more tunnels
little narrow burrows
       hot wax
       burning my fingers

     I'm done
     with you   and
     all you stand for

So tall
like a flower
          a stinging anemone
and I love
your craft
          the deft precision of
your fingers
          the clean channels of
your mind,
but, the world,   my friend
is messy
as am I
honey and pollen   all through
my system
all over   my work bench

and now   I'm done
with you.

DUSTIN JUNKERT

An Empty Tomb

Joseph of Arimathea, hooded and quick, cut
Jesus to pieces and planted Him in fragments
but everywhere whole. On every peak he put
His soul. A finger in the pasture, an ear
under the fig tree, His mighty jaw to the depths
of the sea, His eyes with twine to the back
of a blackbird, the tongue to a nightingale.
Every part by desert by grove, flesh and bone
he gave. But kept the keeping heart his own.

MARIA MELENDEZ

BEHIND EVERY GOOD SOLDIER

It sounds too scripted, unbelievable now,
but he really did ask: what would you think of me

if I killed someone? When this childhood
sweetheart joined the Marines,

I was back from college and leaping at him
for a week or so, smoking at his kitchen window, drinking

in the ridiculous brilliance of a typical
Berkeley garden, azaleas and tropical whatnot.

How sure of greenness it all seemed,
how shocking the mob of growing things

that surged against his little yellow house.
                   —the answer I gave

evaporates, but the question roosts
in the mind's cave, elaborates rubbery wings

each time I meet a returning veteran.
Old lovers, neighbors, boys marching drills

on the college quad, what do I think of you
when I think of you killing?

I see an old ghost, fatigued as storm-
blown sand, standing behind you, and it's

nothing but fangs and finger bones, disguised as a girl
with a sweet little honey-pot country

you've got to defend; she's got her dirty
little hands all over your weapons.

MARIA MELENDEZ

LOVE SONG FOR A WAR GOD

Every part of you contains a secret language.
Your hands and feet detail what you've done.
Your appetite is great, and like the sea,
you constantly advance, lunge after lunge.

Unlike my brother sleeping in his chair,
you do not take reality with ease.
Your pain builds up its body like a cloud
rotating a collage of hot debris.

O Teacher! We have learned that all men's tears
are not created equal. We were wrong
to offer flames to quell your fires. Still,
I must dismember you inside this song.

Your mouth's dark cave awaits Victory's kiss;
blood is the lid your calm eyes never lift.

TO HOPE

for Christian Peacemaker Teams & Langley Hill Friends Meeting

As though sunlight couldn't kill you.

As though sex couldn't kill you.

    As though books had never been covered
              with human skin.

    As though otters thrive in the Tigris.

As though peace lay dormant in marsh mud.

    As though Tom Fox were made of clay
            and could be remade.

If draught, therefore taproot.

    If cracked bridge, therefore bat roost,

pups by June. (If communion

    therefore last supper.) If lasting hunger,

then nightly flights. Half a million

Mexican free-tails flew east, above the river

spiraling out as though they'd never eaten.

MARIA MELENDEZ

AN ARGUMENT FOR THE BRILLIANCE OF ALL THINGS

On a downed spruce at Murie Ranch,
branches curve like scoured whale ribs,
moss adheres as seaweed would.

An old ruffed grouse struts through the windfall,
drumming, drumming
its courtship ritual.

Yet we still hear the claim "human consciousness
consummates," as though matter waits, barren,
for its better half.

Meanwhile, grouse sperm
have every confidence
in the messy interlock

of matter with matter.
If, indeed, consciousness could be
extracted from the mountains

like iron ore, isolated
from shale beds—as crude—siphoned out
from the center of cells

like messenger RNA, could be
examined on a slide plate,
ex situ,

we'd have to admit
that its saline content
matches that of the ocean, a tear,

a teaspoon of semen, a ferning
droplet of amnion waters.
Know this, all humanists:

under the pure, lifeless
surface of the Sea
of Thought swims a great

gray whale, scarred
and barnacled, carrying
a calf, a great gray whale

about to breach.

MARIA MELENDEZ

A DIFFERENT SYMPATHY

If the cord snared
your raw vagina when you pulled
your purple newborn up
to nurse, and every suck was cat-
tongue, nipple smashed, demanding
milk you couldn't make yet
and no one told you, "It's all right,
you will become numb as polished stones,
flow with life," then two days later,
veins in your breasts turned hot-iron hard,
and the magmatic flood of your milk
drenched all your clothes, stank up your room,
stained your bed, and no one told you,
"It's all right, this roar of pain
will soon recede into a trickle,"

and if, on a slow walk,

you saw the river's bulging edge,
where waters gouge troughs
with loyal licking,
where a cow moose's tracks
yield up in grainy swirls
and dissolve,
then you, too, would hunt for reeds,
weave a tiny boat; humming low
old songs, you'd push your son
to root on the breast
of the river.

MARIA MELENDEZ

GOOD NEWS FOR HUMANS

Destruction hasn't been your only story.
All living things beyond you that you've loved,
you've made love live in them: at the junction
of chocolate & cream-colored rings on the king
snake's skin, in the morning sparkle of cows'
dewy slobber all over the pasture, in the powerful
slice of a gator's tail, in the 5 a.m. ruckus
of a capercaillie lek (males squawk and spin, even when
no female's near), in the scraggly herd
of tule elk stepping through patchy fog
in the green coast hills; you've made love
live on the tops of hippos' ever-growing
teeth, and in the osprey's perfect talon-open moment
before splashdown, in the monkey's
soft hair, and in the four toes
on a gray wolf's hidden print; just by noticing
the sparkling blue gem at the dragon's forehead,
you've made love live there, too.

You've placed love on this earth gently as a mother
gorilla puts a baby to her breast.
Thanks to the Academy of Mommies,
especially the Indian elephant ladies
and the lactating grizzlies, you've meted out a fierce,
nutrient love, and it's regal as the guttural purr
of a sleepy lion.

You've even jammed a ladybug-sized love
between the *Homo* and the *sapiens*,

42

meaning love now walks the streets
at all hours.

Thanks to the cinnamon-colored black bear,
you've made a love that flares
beyond categories, love with the snarly strength
of a badger's nose, daring as the gray fox
raising kits under the shed.

You've let love steal
into camp, eat scraps
and piss on leather boots, marmot-style,
and you've let it loose
to twirl and leap in the calls of *Grus
canadensis*. Your love's elastic
as the arms of a praying mantis, and it feeds
backyard suet to the greedy
pine siskin, too tiny
to ever blow anything up. If you can
love a sociopathic cat named Doctor Jesus,
or a tarantula writhing through a secret molt,
you can expect some loving looks
from their creator.

You're sprouted dusty crow wings by this love
that lets you fly to the top of a telephone pole
and perch easy next to the greasy
she-crow with the huge, voluptuous
brain.

Thanks to you, love has the highest view
on top a giraffe's four long
miracles. You've made love undulate,
jungular and oceanic, in tiger
and dolphin music, and you've brought love into the nest

43

of the mountain bluebird. Amor in you,
amor outside of you has been
the old bluetick hound's end-of-driveway howl,
and the growl, too, of the alpha male wolf
under serious threat.

The little loaded springs of love
in your every cell, well, they exploded
and made the fuzzy head and dirty
feet of a little boy:
joy in red overalls, inventing new ways to defeat
gravity, and out of a whole planet worthy
of your dreams, thankfully you've remembered to love especially
the duck-billed platypus.
Thank beastliness!—this love that's made us
claw-hearty, beak-sturdy
enough for life.

AARON J. POLLER

BACK THEN

The strength of family, according to
mother, was an open door. Father

thought otherwise. Some days mother's talk
might never bend. Some days his touch

on the piano would send me far
out of any room. There will be days,

my father said, we entertain alone.

LAURA MCCULLOUGH

HOLY

Weatherman say *snowpocalypse coming,* clear
the stores, duct tape running low, lay some up, iced
tea, twinkies, holy. Make me run, batteries
and cheese, what about some cans? Make them protein
please. Kids in their beds; sky full of dread. Social
*not*working, neighbors all boxed in, this is my
skin you're in. Sorry, autotext bopped
erotic fumble, bobble that snap, snap that
disc; you're out of luck, no scholly for you.
Walk across the street, ring around the moon, some-
thing coming soon and it's better than you, least
live that way. Neighbor crying on the porch, some-
one died today, see the snow, *bon hiver, love,*
goodbye and Snickers are all I got to share.

LAURA MCCULLOUGH

CHANGE THE GAME

Jilly and Rick, meatmasters in the Kingdom
of Loathing, searching for their familiars,
iced White Canadians in hands bricked with
splints; already their wrists are shot, but they don't
know it. The thing is coming any way—*Lux*—not
from the screens, but within, another thing they
don't know, but sense in each other. *Hey Skullhead*,
they croak, push glasses up their nose bridges. Oh,
they are so lovely! Caterpillar brows,
off-the-grid Free People shirt and mismatched
Hush Puppies. *What decade is it now*, they ask.

THE PLURAL OF APOCALYPSE

Yes, there are days   when the bitter saliva
predicts   the early loss of teeth. I am
missing two. Ground until they split.   A
student once told me I needed a tattoo
          for the experience of pain.   Pain.
          I just grinned. Here, it is already the
apocalypse;   you know what I mean.
          Here, I say hope is in an open palm
     like a viral message: maybe today you can
stand. I stand because I am not   alone.
          After the revelation comes the touch:
touch the arm of the boy in the elevator because
you smell his fear;   touch the old man
delivering pizza   as you give him a tip; give
him that tip,   and look in his bleary old
eyes, the sockets sagging from his wife's not yet
death,   but soon, so soon.   It's
raining apocalypses,
          and in the interstices, we find out how we
will behave   ,   wither,   blossom,
          stand   in the day after   a year,
          ten.   You   are not
alone.   Your   prospect   gives   me
aspiration;   my   commitment   helps   her   trust
again; his pleasure kindles the recollection   not
          of what is to come, but of what is possible,
the   ways   we   find   to   go   on: this   plural,   this
preponderance,   profusion,   variety   of   the
living   as well as the beloveds, with us or gone; a

communion of gorgeous   sorrows,   our
reenactment   of the ever falling world; what rains
down, washes us   cleansing us   so   we
can try again.   We all
reveal such pretty   marks.

WE'D LEARN LATER HER HUSBAND LEFT

Though we were young and knew little,
we were good Quakers, and kind, taught
to work in quiet, and when we did talk
to talk from below so that each exchange
took place on a gentle slope, an inclined plane
or pulley system, a simple machine, really,
like one of history's many that's kept
the species ticking. So we ticked along
when Teacher Nancy turned her attention
to somewhere above our heads, a point beyond
us. She cried quietly, and the room shushed
with the soft whisper of safety scissors
that snipped to shape Noah's felt animals.
I—more than most—loved her and wondered
as I cut who I could hurt to stop her hurt,
sure that some violence God could endorse,
that mercy's counterweight is just
and swift. That I, in my kindness, must deliver it.

ADAM HOULE

SOMNILOQUENCE ON THE HIGH PLAINS

When dreams rise from your familial past
of tongue-speakers seared in Holiness
I listen for some sense in the gamboling
vowels and consonants as they spill
from the headwaters of your lips.
The Pentecostal Spirit enflames you.
Come daybreak, you are drawn and wan,
changed, the way Oklahoma's red dust
must have stained the hand-spun hems
of dresses worn by the stalk-thin women
you weigh yourself against, reckoning
nightly in your attic glossolalia a faith
that compels you to seek more rousing fires,
first through grace then by sore travails.
Wet your brow. The lenient city admits you now
from off night's furnace of creosote and shale.

ADAM HOULE

CHIHUAHUA NATIVITY SCENE

And why the hell not
cast in porcelain three wise dogs?
Joseph is a Chihuahua, and the angel
that oversees this miracle
from a crow's nest atop the manger
is a Chihuahua, haloed and grinning.
The shepherds are Chihuahuas
that clutch in doggy paws their golden
shepherds' crooks. Mary's good
donkey is a dog. The camel is a dog.
Mary her blue-clad self is an eggshell
dog, and the Bradford Exchange's newly
minted Prince of Peace, a human baby,
doesn't appear concerned at all.

MARIAN KAPLUN SHAPIRO

QUAKER MEETING: CAMBRIDGE/RANGELEY, MAINE

There you are, purchasing
    the Sunday paper. Ibuprofen.
        Ajax. Pampers. Peanut butter.
            Margarine. Clorox. There
you are, baby squalling, holy
    voices in the IGA,
        in Sarah's kitchen tasting oatmeal-
        raisin bread, yearning
for pies and chocolate frosting. You
    will not forget the Wednesday corn
        line. You must choose: How
            many? and are the kernels
small and sweet?

        "Almost died," he
said, "fever of 106, down to
the hospital." "Going to rain, trees
need the water, I guess." "Thanks be
to God, my son got out, the night my store
burned down." "Geologist dug up this
here rock, said it was from the time
of the Grand Canyon. Used to be this land
was all under water, back then."
"Learned me the Internet at
the library—looked up my condition
on the Medline, they call it. Ain't
no reason, just old age, they say, doctors
don't know, but I'd have gone blind, it said,
if they hadn't of given me the Cortisone

in time." "I'll think on it awhile, let
you know if I can fix it for you." "The locksmith
out Rt. 4, he was a Baptist preacher,
died last June, you know. The schoolbus driver
he's out 16 across from where the diner was,
the widow sold him all the molds. Lock
stock and barrel, you could say." "Those wasps
you got, just spray 'em with Raid and run
like hell."

ERROL HESS

UNBUILDING

Beginning with the house,
first removing its comforts
we once built up piece by piece,
stripping it down to bare utility,
to stark walls, and, on the floor,
just a stove, refrigerator, table, chair,
a mat to sleep on.

Next go the windows, the floor itself
and ceiling, all doors,
then we tear down its walls, block by block,
till only corners enough are standing
to hold the roof and give wind some little shelter.

I teach my children now to hide
from the sight of a stranger,
to grab loose things of value
set down too far from their owners,
to beg shamelessly with full pockets
and to find warmth and laughter
in the nooks and windfall shelters of their world.

We give up the house altogether.

BIRD SHADOWS

Winter birds, circling,
cast long shadows swift
across a wind-swept field.

All on the ground is brown,
bitten down by winter wind,
except for sage grass clumps standing

too close to blow, too soft to break.
The topmost vulture
turns on a stationary wing,

hangs still in stiff wind,
looks down on kettling kin,
on three mockingbirds chasing

a red tail hawk trying to
follow the ramped air upward,
on an old man cleaning last summer's

garden of dead tomato vines.
A bright day, long shadows
weave over ground the human works

to clean; the wind drives scraps
tumbling across, catching against
composting piles of wood mulch,

against car tires, tomato stakes, legs.
The vulture twists, flips a wingtip
feather, kites on upward.

TUOL SLENG

in memory of the 18,000

So too rust infects
the chain link coils of bed springs
stilled beneath the body where metal
presses to ribs.

In spots of nowhere the prisoner's hands
disappear, arm twisted
into camera view.

Children of death I feel your eyes
like a million glass vases
reflecting some false sun.

I want to give you birds
hovering at the harsh cement, a slow dream
before falling.

The spaces between the first and last
photographs are an open cell stained,

the gut smell of trenches filled
like rivers unmoving

over which they carry
only seven
through the unchained doors
and the sky flickers open, poison in the wound.

ANDREA ENGLAND

REMEMBERING SLEEP, THEN WAKING

I knew I was dreaming when the baby turned
from my breast and only the liquor store carried
formula. Surrounded by packing boxes
and want ads I remembered the rubric
of the imagination, that some things
we must experience before dreaming
them. In high school, waking just before
consummation was everything.

After sleep my body is warm and sticky
like the baby. I lie next to what I know.
When the body fails the mind it fails
the heart. What's left then, are drive-by
landscapes and barb-wired highways casketing
the deer and acacia by our own design.

INDISTINGUISHABLE

The brothers rise to the silver glint of twilight, acres of unharvest between them, swing their legs over the sides of their beds in unison remembering the heavy arc of hay bailing, and the redness of steel pitchforks resurrected as blisters between their calloused hands. It was an impossible spring, planters sunk in the fields, seeds rotting or springing up stunted or in the wrong row like displaced stars. Now it's November and the brothers bow and shake their high foreheads. They've wrung their bodies of this work but they wake anyway, one braving the snow-studded driveway to the other's. They've downsized, both their wives dead now, they can be brothers again. One asks the other will he bring him his gray woolen fedora. They sit holding hands like new lovers. The older brother points to six young men in swimming trunks in a chorus line. It's 1939, the World Fair stilled in the background. One asks the other, *Do you remember that summer?* His brother replies, *Of course I do. I was there. Wasn't I?*

ELLEN WEHLE

SECOND COMING

He for whom we set an extra place at table.

On the eve of bombardment

Rumors fly: Stalin himself, come to rescue his city.

How terrible our thirst, how patient,

Excalibur at lake-bottom. In Rome, a coroner

Clicks off the mic as weeping

Gangsters crowd the room, hound-like, licking their master's

Incisions. Whom we await. His field of force. Christ

Sighted doling out bread, *No*, someone

Else says, *Sandbagging like any soldier, down by the docks.*

ELLEN WEHLE

FRAGMENT FROM QUMRAN

It's no secret lovemaking smells
        Of the sea because sinking into each

Other's bodies we return to a briny
        Beginning, that Eden lay underwater.

As for the lode of iron ore threading
        Our veins, only consider how comets

Journey bearing us gifts, how muck-
        Hole to mountain we crawled ashore,

Code cached like rubies inside our
        Bones. Wind-worn, silvered, planks

Half-foam half-gone, that gate still
        Shutting the legion waves behind us.

ELLEN WEHLE

ALL SOULS' DAY

Start with a fact: the New England town
I moved to, fiery leaves

Caught under an iron fence. Practicing
Death we stay

In bed. Here is the churchyard, each stone
Glowing. Colonial

Houses disappear over hilltops, sumacs toss
Scarlet dresses

Onto the pyre. Stripped down to bone, we
Offer ourselves instead.

ELLEN WEHLE

TRUTH

Pipes knocking
All winter, we
Heard echoes.

Some sparrow
Caught in mind's
Crawlspace.

What we chose
Not to know
Dropped coins

Off the overpass
Until cursing we
Swerved. As if

We could ditch
Our own party.
Donkey piñatas

Swaying blindly
To what splits
Us, what comes

Tapping in those
Hours our sleep
Begs the blow.

ELLEN WEHLE

TRUTH

Accrued by inches,
Moonlight lapping
Casement sills.

Refused once
Decanted to slip
Back in her bottle.

Stray cat keening
In our yard, we
Walked out into

Wilderness, lamps
Aloft to find her—
Unmappable tract

Within the ribcage,
Cry followed so
Far and yet farther—

Afterwards the dust
Settled, broken
Glass swept up, we

Carved her eye above
Doorways, gaze
Leveled like a blade.

OUT OF THE SILENCE

On First Day a man stood up and said
"Our task, Friends, is to be worthy
of what we were spared for!" That's all

the man said, and failed to explain what
he had in mind or provide any context.
I have heard lines like that in the street

or in bars, and assumed they were uttered
by those who were half insane, perhaps
some bearded fool muttering to himself.

But then again, there might be a context
one does not speak of, for it's odd how
life and light waver, how one is spared

or is not—the diagnosis outlived or war
survived or the dread nuclear nightmare
delayed far beyond probabilities although

there's nothing on earth not hostage still.
The man rose to his feet on First Day—
a morning that had somehow arrived

as promised, grace enough. But another
war was in progress and each day's evil
more than sufficient to balance its blessings.

DAVID RAY

DOING WITHOUT

's an interesting
custom, involving such in-
      visible items as the food
that's not on the table, the clothes
      at are not on the back
the radio whose music
      is silence. Doing without
is a great protector of reputations
      since all places one cannot go
are fabulous, and only the rare and
      enlightened plowman in his field
or on his mountain does not overrate
      what he does not or cannot have.
Saluting through their windows
      of cathedral glass those restaurants
we must not enter (unless like
      burglars we become subject to
arrest) we greet with our twinkling
      eyes the faces of others who do
without, the lady with the
      fishing pole, and the man who looks
amused to have discovered on a walk
      another piece of firewood.

DAVID RAY

HAVING TOO MUCH

shows in more places, not
only the face but the belly and
the polished leather. Wher-
ever you go, round every port
of call, folks who practice
this custom walk with cameras
knocking their knees and
genitals. Like busybodies
they have so many friends to
look in on they never quite
catch up. They must use
boats, planes, rockets, upon
which they distribute
cigarettes like tickets that
will glow and take you
anywhere, even to the
moon when it opens up
for the season. What they
have learned is certain lessons
which they are fond of
citing, e.g. *money talks*
and they appear to be in despair
from never absorbing quite
enough electricity.

DAVID RAY

PAPA HEMINGWAY

Sometimes I imagine him
as coming back
the way my father should have.

Or maybe I could find Papa
in the diner and think of myself
as Nick, sent on the famous errand,

the one that made the Swede
tremble in his rooming house
so much like where my father

lived the year he sweated
night shift in a Kansas smelter.
There is no way, I am quite sure

that either papa could once again
tread this earth or greet me.
And yet I'm often on alert

like those who look around
for God or gold, or expect some
ecstatic rapture that can never be.

HEIDI HART

THE GOLDEN HOUR

On the plane, the radiologist explains
the gap between head trauma and

salvation or oblivion: one
fluorescent, bloodied hour

of imaging and sounding, waves
in three dimensions as

machines hum, drip, and beep,
split seconds, dendrites

forked in lightning dream and what
might be the spirit lightening the body

as it lifts and hovers and
returns, or not. I'm flying toward

the city I am leaving, temporary
body, valley ringed with stone

and snow. This hour. The lake agleam.

MARYHELEN SNYDER

SUN IN AN EMPTY ROOM

for Edward Hopper

A single figure sits at the round table.
   The loneliness thing has been overdone

wrote Hopper. *It formulates something you don't want*
   formulated. Not because you are keeping a secret,
     but because light is everywhere, even

at night, and something we will never name is looking.
   Something sees her hat and her ungloved hand
     holding the white cup at the Automat,

the precise bend of his body as he sits alone on the curb
   on a Sunday. Sees how the 11 AM window light
     meets her in the exact moment

of her eyes' reaching. Feels how light looks on the side
   of a lone house—and paints *that light.*

Today the air is filled with rain not quite falling.
   The autumn leaves cry for attention in the way
     of light in a dark room. Their colors

are Hopper's. The russets and pale yellows,
   the golds and greens. When the artist is looking,
     nothing is lonely.

*

No two people in any Hopper painting
          are meeting each other eye to eye.
                    These, on their porch in their canvas chairs

are gazing out toward the sea. Not touching.
          Not speaking. Not rising to make tea.
                    Not leaving the silence between them.

Who is she, his wife who is the model for every woman
          who looks nothing like her? After they married
                    she began making notations of her own

in the notebooks he kept on each painting. Under
          his careful pencil sketch of *Summertime,*
                    she writes *large strong woman*

in thin white dress. She does not say, *her round breasts*
          naked under the cloth, the flesh of her thigh
                    shining. Elsewhere

his newspaper leans on the table between them as he reads.
          Turning her body toward their upright piano, she rests
                    her elbow on that table that links them

and touches softly a single note with her finger.
          Or considers touching.
                    Comes close.

*

He is eighty now. This is almost his last.
          He changes his mind about a figure.
                    He allows empty. Empty

of everything except light. Standing before it,
        I am most moved. And there
                on the floor of this room which holds

only the one painting is the figure, the young girl
        sketching the painting in charcoal
                with great concentration.

What are you after here, they had asked him
        regarding the empty room, regarding the sun.
                I am after me, he had answered.

There is light on the head of the young girl
        and on the white page filling now with
                her seeing what he saw.

MARYHELEN SNYDER

LAMB OF THE CATALINAS

My eyes on the heavy-lidded eye of the Lamb,
I drive down the long avenue through Tucson
to the base of the Catalinas, now turning pink,
to the place where I laid your ashes handful
by handful under the eye of the Lamb,

the eye looming larger as I drive, then vanishing
into the stone face and fragmenting into the many rocks
it actually is. I walk up the same path
I walked a year ago to the place where I stood
holding the remains of you close to my chest

as though you were my child. I am eager
to get to you, to plop myself down in the center
of where I threw you to earth and wind, circling
around to give you to all of the valley, all of the hills,
eager to sit now as though in your lap as the sun

turns the giant saguaros into red supplicants, and mixes
new blues on the palate of the sky. I did not imagine
the peace I would feel in your presence, now
that you are part of the earth, nor can I remember
exactly how I lost it, each little fragment of memory

seeming not enough to explain how I could crumble
against the stones you piled up around you. Yet
in those last years of your gradual decay when
I would bathe you, allowing the soft wet cloth
to be the way I could touch every part of your body

that had brought me into this life, I loved you
very precisely, the straight small nose, the flat
scarred chest where your breasts had been, the rounded belly
that has lived on through generations of us, past
the bearing of our children. I could move the soapy cloth

over your thighs, into the folds of your vulva. But love
is too simple a word for even a moment of what
I felt with you, blood-bound as though with the old cord,
yet guarded against you, a convoluted animal
shrinking into its own bones, even when your breaking brain

could no longer remember the reasons for your fury at me,
and even when in those last years your joy in me
became child-like, lighting you up each time I walked
into your room, no matter how briefly gone.
When you were still alive, even that light

frightened me, as though it claimed me. But
in this light, this summer evening, I do not remember
in my body how fear feels. Soon I will be walking
back to the place where we talk about mothers.
Perhaps I will tell them again how you betrayed me.

But here every darkening stone and leaf, the intricate ground
where your bone chips mingle with millions of years
of shattered matter, cry out their innocence. Forgiveness
is irrelevant where now the first stars bring word
of the nameless watching benignly with its indefinable eye.

MARYHELEN SNYDER

THE LESSON

for Stanley Plumly

Settling into worship we Quakers call it, into
waiting for light. We sit at a long table,
wide windows chronicling winter's early dark.
When the light speaks, I write it in my book
as though I had not heard it before

and am at risk of forgetting. *Stop being poets;
it's useless. The poem has to teach you.*
And this: *Be as Severn with Keats.* The last weeks
of Keats' life, Severn's is a lone watch. Both
are barely grown to manhood and far from home.

The heaves of death are enormous now,
the consumption thick with mucous
and clotted blood. Between spasms of choking,
the poet sleeps. To keep himself awake,
Severn sketches Keats's brow, still wet.

Neither a death mask nor a mask that life wears,
this face, which cannot see itself, is pure beauty.
The slight down turn of the lips when
there is no one to please. The brow washed clean
over his *teeming brain.* An unseen candle

casting a dark halo. The bend of his head
on the pillow toward the beholder.
If Keats's eyes were open, we would see how

he takes his beholder for granted now, for grace.
Keats knows he is dying, no matter how

Severn protests. *Be like Keats with Severn.*
Dying. The artist outlives the poet long enough
to imitate even his last imitation, to say
I have lived too long on his own deathbed.
Be as Keats. Trusting the watch.

LAUREN RUSK

BUILDING DOWN

"We're building down," my neighbor said.

    Gutting the basement
                    in surgical masks
they pry the plywood off—
       skreeling groans
                as nails
        lose their grip—
bash the concrete back to rubble,
rend the fibrous trash,
and at last lay bare
          the stilts,
   too spindly
to keep on holding
          the storied hulk…

Under hardwood:
   splinters, expired
     permits,
  crawl space
        black
   widow city.

              Flung out,
a rusted rollerskate.

   Sandal-style like mine, at eight—

the magic
            of ball bearings—

a footprint,
            telescoping,
                        with my own
skate key!

                        It's
not the where
            (up and down the block)

but the going—
      rush
            of motion and rust,
chattering over the cracks.

JANICE MILLER POTTER

PSALM FOR APPALACHIA

Turning shifts for decades, he left a chair by the door
where he tied and untied the broken laces in his boots.

The pencil-marked white table hosts his dinner bucket
whose lid should clank it another dent, whose waxed

paper is balled up for the garbage. But he's left that.
Damp as dug coal, the night has hauled out hard scrabble.

Shirring and bounding, crickets clear weeds and grass.
A moth-eaten beam passes over the room and shatters

the table and the ladderback chair, coal-stained as a lung.
In the skillet, soot marls the sickly white bacon grease

left for a supper of fried eggs which never break.
Nobody is coming back. Nobody is ever coming back.

JANICE MILLER POTTER

OUR BOOTS KEPT WANTING TO MELD

I.

Out-of-towners often wondered about the odd smell
lingering over the blackened valley. "It's the smell
of money," my cousin's grandfather would quip.

The smoke ran like water across the wooded hills
rising from the hollow of the Monongahela
fifty-seven years ago, a weather inversion having

forced down dense spumes of smoke and soot
from Donora's zinc and steel mills, back down
the throats of animals, humans, tomato patches,

steep acres of deciduous forests, gray in an hour.
Even so, the Saturday football game punted on,
high on a hill where the fans could see the plays

while down in the hollow people were gasping
for breath, choking, and vomiting up their blood
in houses hardly a stone's throw from the mills.

Before the weather lifted, they counted twenty
people dead. No one counted the grizzled dogs,
matted in wet smoke, red-tongued and stiffened

beside their chains. Or the links of burnt hillsides,
aerially photographed out of a morbid curiosity
but not for visceral evidence before a sootless court.

Oddly, the hills and that hollow have not disappeared
from the face of the earth. They are the earth now,
just a few miles from home, down the road skirting

the Monongahela, where we drove countless nights
after dark, slowly, mesmerized by the waterfire of coke
ovens, snaking along molten-orange river and skies.

II.

Our boots kept wanting to meld into the muck
during one clearing late-autumn day, after a fretful
week of thunderstorms, decades after the devastation.

Foot-sore of resistance, we passed a moment
on a little knoll, looking back across the fields
bared for winter. With his usual concern,

my father's squint gathered in his nine cattle,
propped like roan miniatures on the opposite rise.
But I, an out-of-towner for a scatter of years,

could not perceive with his pastoral pleasure.
From where I stood, my view fastened onto
an invisible mine fire seaming under his land,

its smoke perpetually turning up a corner of field
by the hedgerow and the road, where the cattle
could, but never did seem to, trundle a cowpath.

Unlike me, he'd known the mills and coal mines
inside out, known the buried smell of his money
had gotten me away. When he'd caught his breath,

82

we trudged on, I absently watching his denim arm
fan arcs of winter ryeseed across the slant hillside,
the ovules catching onto his roughened hand,

leaving ochre flecks of husk and germ among deep
chapped crevices, bluish veins, and ashen hairs.
Whereas, according to deed, he was sole possessor

of these twenty surface acres, companies owned
all the underground, disaster-immune, in perpetuity.
How deep was his, I wondered. Six feet. One inch.

For exploitation, for the tragic remains, for his
buttonless sleeve, where is the hollow of lament?
Like a boy from a far-gone era, earning his nickel

peddling newspapers, he had slung a canvas sack
across his chest. From its quiver, he sowed handful
after handful of seed across his drabbled fields,

feeding them with winter nitrogen that, sooner
or later, would turn a blanket of bluegreen blades
for all the tears that had fed and gullied this land

down to a balding skull, flesh-thin, with grass.

SIBYL RUTH

FULL HOUSE

Surrounded by stubborn furniture,
all yours.

Double-sided bookcases,
stacks of little tables.
Oak cabinets, sideboards, cupboards.
The uncomfortable chaise longue,
an out-of-tune piano.

Pieces glower from every corner.
Obstructing windows,
they cast odd shadows,
darken doorways.

There's plenty of room, you say.
I could make the occasional gesture with a duster.
Be more accommodating.

While they graze my shins for fun
snag sleeves, tweak fingernails,
nip my vulnerable toes.
And they won't be moved.

I'd imagined owning less.
Somewhere unvarnished, uninsured
—bare walls and floors,
with wind chimes, maybe lanterns.
Stars looking down on a shared emptiness.

ANN RITTER

GRANDFATHER: 1932

The way is not paved,

the three miles that you walk

for work, your long leg bones

flute-like, hips sockets grinding.

In the spring you pull out

your two front teeth

on the bottom that a dentist

has numbed from pain

three days before,

flinging them, useless,

into a gray

rut of sand

on the road.

ESTHER GREENLEAF MURER

QUAKERS AND THE ARTS: A HISTORY

Quakers and artists
meeting as oil and water
for three hundred years.

Christ the True Substance
makes our vain imaginings
brewing of soma.

Solomon Eccles
smashed his viols, burned his music—
one less composer.

Catherine Phillips,
called to vocal ministry,
stopped writing verses.

D. Fox's cello
lies buried in the garden;
there it does no harm.

Players and pipers,
we that walk disorderly,
limners and rhymers—

Wanton diversions
distract us from the Kingdom,
promote a light mind.

We are grasshoppers,
fiddling while ants prize their time,
mending the world's wounds.

ESTHER GREENLEAF MURER

BETWEEN

Numbers 9:15–23

And so you bid me leave this place behind.
But whether I shall journey south or north,
Or what new labors I am meant to find,
You will not tell me. Only venture forth!
To learn to wander well, this is the task:
To follow step by step as I am led,
Steer my course by fire and cloud, nor ask
More than the daily manna for my bread.

But now imperiously the clouds descend,
Erase the skyline, curtain off the distance,
And laze about my tent for months on end
Until I scarce can credit the existence
Of aught beyond my hand. Meanwhile this stone
That tripped me up has beauties all its own.

PHYLLIS HOGE

THE LIGHT ON THE DOOR

Something about that old house we passed
In the last town. Orleans? Coventry?
The door with the long glass oval.
The pale light, failing light, canted on the blind surface,
The glow from the bevel rainbowed,
Caved in on time, on history.

Nothing in nature so catches at the well of sadness
As this. Nothing. Not evocative mist
Slow-wreathing through budded woodlands,
Not breeze-blown rippling lake water as it laps ashore,
Not warm violets shaded,
Not airy honeysuckle lattice.

This pang can come anywhere. What is the reason? I suppose
Such light, lilac, slopes across lives almost ours
That we didn't have—a weight
As of a slumbering presence within the walls
Of old houses, an immanence
Brooding. What we longed for.

Almost as if we could open the burnished door,
Step into a hallway, a rose-dark room with high ceiling,
And, looking out from the other side
Through wavery glass of a tall window, find life in a lost year,
Old sunlight, rung chimes. Shimmer
Of the possible. Out of reach. Ours.

TWO PHOTOGRAPHS

This day, purified to nude, could be the past
Released. The light does not shift: it holds.
Sleet glazes the roads and slate roof-tiles,
And, falling through spread branches of the pines,
Drains even their needles to ice-green celadon.
The afternoon reduces to an old photograph,
Black and white, glassy, its world inward
And without reference, self-reflecting silver, monochrome.

And in this early picture you are standing
In another year, another morning,
Written in the brightness of hours off the water
And coastal-shale near Beavertail Lighthouse,
Smiling for the camera. Shades of the one tone
Illuminate your face, your young body,
But no one can read in your eyes the monochrome
Of the life you will have. It's hidden behind glasses.

Immanent in the past, the future rests photographed
And unrecognizable. I, who clicked the shot,
Could see through a lens the living image
Of my desire, and I did not know it.
Latent, it lay hidden in a film, caught up
In its loss, saved there, self-sufficient, as I was,
Until time proved the negative, and this day came, fixed,
Silvery, fallen from a past found in a transparency,

Where we will stay as long as the light does not change.

The First Word

there was still time
before we gave names to days and to seasons
counted hours on clocks
numbered the brief years
the centuries as they fell

there was still time
before we made measures
squares, straight lines, arcs, circles
numbers
when only the surging-everywhere winds
suggested how barren the world was
outside the caves

there was a silence

there was still time

almost to know the thing in itself—
rabbit, mole, spider, tree

afterwards, never—

WHAT WE GIVE

After he'd been imprisoned twenty-one years
On Robben Island, authorities transferred
Nelson Mandela to a concrete bastion
From whose bare walled-in roof a man could see
Only the sun-filled sky.
                              Missing the ocean,
The familiar grass and trees, the salt sea wind,
He asked for and was given sixteen oil drums
Cut in half, dirt filled, to plant a garden
On the roof. In his wide-brimmed straw hat
He worked his thirty-two plots two hours daily.
His harvested spinach and beans he gave away,
And lettuce, strawberries, carrots, aubergines,
Cucumbers, broccoli, peppers, tomatoes, beets—
Some to the warders, some to his friends,
Some to the common-law prisoners.

We give what we have. For the next six years
Of his prison term he gave time and labor.

We give what we have, give what we have too much of,
Give what we've made for pleasure of the making.
Sometimes we give what someone needs. Sometimes
Because of our need to be received we offer
Tokens of who we are. We have an ache
To be given, called desire, called lettuce leaves,
Called love tended in prison.

PAMELA MURRAY WINTERS

IN WHICH I AM MAD AT FLOWERS
BECAUSE PAUL IS DYING

The iris was drooping by the steps when I found it,
ripped, roots and all, from a neighbor's yard.

I carried it to work, filled an old bottle from the tap,
stuck it in. Its inner petals—they're called *standards*,

a friend told me—lay in a heap. Arranging them
with index nudges, I wondered whether I did damage,

as with a butterfly or fledgling. But you can't damage
what's already dead, I guess. Forty minutes later,

it rises from the green bottleglass, standards perked,
the lower petals—called the *fall*—splayed like hands

of some cartoon alien, purple with impossibly
delicate lifelines on sun-yellow palms. Looking at it,

limber, succulent, seemingly self-possessed,
rattles the shards under my ribs, where easy love once was.

PAMELA MURRAY WINTERS

THE LIMITS OF CULTURE

A thirty-year-old man was brought to us
from the field hospital three days after
his platoon, on patrol, drove over
an improvised explosive device (Figure 1).
Amputations and debridement were performed.
Samples were taken, and clinical doses
of drugs were delivered to his mouth and,
later, when dehydration set in, his veins.

Cultures were run in three separate laboratories
far from the field. Studies revealed
a new variety of sporulating fungus.
Death calls to life, and in the empty places
the authors found these flowers,
framed in slender dishes (Figure 2).

These were assayed and identified as
beauty that could not find a root
in metal and therefore yearned sunward
from the place he kept his wallet, the place
his savior bled, the place he waved goodbye.

The pathogen was found too late for antifungal measures.
The family requested palliative treatment.
The isolate, a member of the order Mucorales,
was named for the field where it moved
from soil to flesh (Figure 3).

Figure 1. Earth knows what man cannot.

Figure 2. "Flowers are better than bullets."

Figure 3. A roadside in Kabul.

FERMENTATION

When the growing season ends, we make sauerkraut.
Mom shreds the cabbage, knife rasping against
tightly layered leaves. Then she adds salt and whey,
pounds everything until it bruises and weeps, and
shoves the limp cabbage into a quart jar.
She screws the lid on tight.

Every now and then, I go to the basement and
check on the sauerkraut. I peer through the glass
jar and see little bubbles. Sometimes they rise to
the surface as I watch. The brine seeps out
beneath the lid and trickles down the sides,
pooling on the floor. Inside, the cabbage
is steeping, changing, becoming.

New wine, Jesus said, and surely he knew
about dark, cool silence, the sour smell
of ripening. But he also knew how life breaks
the seal and comes bursting out one morning,
green and pungent, fresh with salty
tang on its lips.

MARTIN WILLITTS, JR.

HOW TO BE SILENT

Into the evening and beyond, swooping
nightjars chase moths. The sound of them,
less than silence, is hush
spiraling. If this be the color of tree bark,
then what are those long tipped wings
sliding across the moorlands out of the brackens
with no more noise than a prayer kept to yourself?
They concealed themselves from daylight,
and now they are after the large flying insects,
like there is no tomorrow. And they should know
belonging more to darkness than to the known,
moving with suddenness. Into the evening
and beyond, where light is already disappearing,
are whispers of sounds that are less than whispers.
We want to reduce things into simple things.
Into a bird touching silence. We want distilled silence—
to reach into that speechless sense of wonder.
We want to suppress those things that worry at our bones.
But those darting nightjars, smothering darkness,
stopping sounds into nothingness, they shush the stars.
They make the quiet possible with their presence.
They put an end to things that move in night.
They encourage silence into happening.

ST. JOHNS, OREGON, SOON AFTER MY GRANDFATHER'S DEATH

One afternoon I went down
to the Columbia and watched
the hazy ships
carrying their cargo to the skeletal cranes
of steel shipping yards.

The sunlight kept on, for a while.
The crickets were still finding their harmony.
The gorge was smeared with color.
My father caught his breath and said
All this, and heaven too?

I could see even then
that my eyes were clouding.
Weeks later the lenses would be perched
on the bridge of my nose,
to push the world beyond my face
into some kind of focus.

Soon that day the separations blurred,
the sun faded, and darkness became the color
of everything. My father walked me back
to the house while I trailed his hand,
in love with the sound
of my footsteps, and he
softly said *The cherry trees
will blossom very soon. See?*

A STATUE OF A SAINT

He walked for miles
among the hazelnut trees.

Over and over he repeated Basho:

Even in Kyoto,
hearing the cuckoo's cry,
I long for Kyoto.

The rain fell thick
and heavy like a weeping statue

of a saint, like a dog drooling
in heat,

like a cuckoo spitting
blood.

> Your shirt is torn,
> hungry eyes, and bare

> feet. I'm hungry too.

> Take this bread.

He walked for hours
in the dark

wooden rooms of his mother's house.

The clock chimed. Creatures

too small for sight wondered
at the sound.

      Your Sunday suit is stained;
      empty, hungry eyes. A cross

      of ash on your forehead.

      The holes worn in the knees
      of your jeans.

MIKE McGEEHON

AFTER WATCHING *THE THIN RED LINE*

for my dead students

War is blister on a hillside.
War is fought by scared children
who fight scared children.

War is a student who loved
art more than saw mills,
who joined up to pay for school

and watched his best friend's
leg vaporize, who held him
more tenderly than any lover

while the medic pumped morphine
into the emptiness left behind.
War is my student coming home

too angry to paint, re-upping
to be with his friends again.
War is a man writing a poem

in a lush green land, pretending
he knows what children know
while they die in a desert.

MIKE MCGEEHON

PASTOR PLAYS HOOKY

for Peggy Senger-Biko

Sometimes the sunshine wins,
the creak of hot leathers
cooled by speed, the world

sprinting past as you weave
through the Sunday traffic.
And sometimes the sweet smell

of the seed grass turning
from green to gold wins
and the drone of an engine

humming your whole body
beats out the hard pews
and hymns sung off key.

It's not a sin to leave your
flock in the hands of God,
especially when the sprinklers

in the long back fields are
misting up the asphalt,
bringing a sweet relief.

KEJT WALSH

AN APPRECIATION

In the rainstorm, I'm standing
in my gray coat like a plastic
stopper in the bathtub. In the swirl
of water I am still. The moss clinging
to wetted tree trunks swells
and spreads while the brick
of the library wears to a sheen.
This storm is foreign. In Florida
all storms were violence. Crows thrashed
on the power lines when the heavy rains
beat concrete. The tops of palm trees lifted
in the wind and came down, leaving spiky
posts shorn of deadened crowns.
The sky was always a menacing pink, stained
from gases that choked in the lungs.
Now I linger in the dark breath
of this new kind of storm.

KRISTIN CAMITTA ZIMET

YARN FOR BOSNIA

Some nerve-jangled imp or claw-hook cat
turned these hanks that lay smooth—
gray lambs, bassinet babies, risen loaves—
into a snarl that spills over the table,
smoke curling thick over a ruined town.

Women in Bosnia, pulling free
out of the wreckage lives tangled and split,
bits of blanket and mangled coats,
rolling the ruin up, as women do,
ask us for yarn. For them I begin

rewinding what I have, making a wad
the size of a newborn fist, dancing it back
out of loosening knots, up-gathering
into a soft globe, moving the overlap
so that it spirals out, the center everywhere.

Out of this skein my mother knit
an afghan my grandmother held,
white doves against gunmetal grey,
a coverlet for comfort as she died;
her fingers hugged the loops,

her family intact, one generation
snugged into the next, the long yarn
without hitch. Sisters, tie on your lot
to mine. I want to hear your needles
click, counting, casting on.

KRISTIN CAMITTA ZIMET

PRAYER MEETING

Neither public charity nor private room,
our cases are collected in this ward
where silver runners bend above each bed,
short curtains whisking each of us from sight,
or halfway out. We glance aside;
words, like our street clothes, have been hung away.
The trousers of the doctors, bending down,
the screek of crank and rail,
hint at what intimate, undignified exam
visited upon our neighbors now
comes to us next. Below each sober face,
out of the skimpy gown, there poke
the splinted arm, the feeding tube,
the bag of waste, the breathing hole
in the throat. It is easy to divine
what gurgles and pours,
what loss is coded on each secret chart.
Days, one sigh passes from mouth to mouth
down the whole row. Nights, one mantra moan
rolls voice to voice until she clatters in,
the midnight minister, the cart of meds.
To every sheet is clipped the button that connects
to the lit station down the hall
where call lights flash together
and on a single shelf our monitors
jump to the various lightnings of the heart.

SOMETHING'S FALLING

Because, and here's my point,
because now, because loosened
by small destructions, because
shrapnel of civilization down
dizzy slow, because a little hand
drowning. Something's falling.
Because empires of our beliefs
could inherit us promised days
but something's falling. Now,
because we summon armies and
thugs unoriginal, barter a future
placid for a present spooked,
something's falling because weary
apples weary, over and again.

Because only history supports
as we rant at kids on stick-
trembling legs, weep on fallow
chests, join neighbors one to
a four-cornered sheet stretched
to break the inevitable, study
a sky's hindsight: Should it have
loosened more rain, moisting drops
to shimmer oily in sun, adorned
itself nirvanic swim-pool
aquamarines it's marveled over
or painted indigo paisleys of a Hindu
bride across its breathy canopy?

Because what else? Recode
the Rosetta of history? Or will
love to our ones as cool heat
lifts soothing to the viridian
moss out of reach but scudding
close still, because the drowning
little hand, little hand, can touch it.

SARAH SARAI

A RHETORICAL INQUIRY INTO THE MORAL CERTITUDE OF CAUSE AND EFFECT

Today we picked tulips and
stubbed our big toe and went
to war and lost a bunch a arms
and feet and shit and gunned
down a dozen fifty people
and got tired and took a nap
and had a family and raised
a mess a kids and picked
daffodils and scratched our
finger bad and then we went
to war. We blew up some big
stuff and little stuff and people
tall and stupid crying babies
and a whole lot a us puked
and we were buried or they
put us on these lame cots and
we got better and met girls
and boys and had families and
glued pink fuzzy bunny ears
on our sister's headband for
spring assembly and then we
killed a whole lot more people
cause we had to go to war cause
we picked lilies and sneezed and
after you pick lilies and sneeze
or something they send you to
war. Don't you know anything?

SARAH SARAI

REMORSE

When he lumbered in the way of men
who use their hands to till earth,
he knocked a rough doorway
and sobbed for unfairness and
the slaying. Dull, trembling,
he threw on three pelts against
a desert night, and feared heaven's
white stars. We've all killed our brother.
The dead roam through us.
We toss beneath old gods' blazing navigation.
Cain? It's morning. He bites a sweet seedy fig.

RICHARD MARX WEINRAUB

A VISION AT THE QUAKER SCHOOL

The avatar who'd be my love was born
in 1965 while I was drowning
in a sea of tables near Poughkeepsie.
Uranus and the double planet
Pluto were conjunct. His mother was the world

erupting—clothing him in golden
skin to save us from the mean master. The moon
and Mercury were trine—the trinity
of God becoming what I fancied:
Vishnu's son, the boarish Varaha.

The only way to beat the devil
is to have horns, too. Tusks lifted Earth from black
waters upon a plate. He held a lotus,
conch, and cudgel in three hands; and with his fourth
he offered me a ring—of Saturn squared.

TO BIND A WOUND

She undressed me.
Unwound the wound
Behind the question.
I was displayed.
My nudity was white,
Malleable, mutable.

Now when I ask
I am a lump of clay.
Or metal melted down
To amorphousness.

Amoeba-like, hands
Pray for structure,
Work the wheel, wield
The clay that is a purpose,
The shape behind the shape
That is my hand.

I build breasts and thighs
Of a woman.
A form that moves with mind
To bind a wound.
A wound dressed with a question,
Made whole by decision: seize love.

JUDY RAY

TIME ON MY HANDS

I draw the splayed hand, time ticking
at the wrist. Broad, peasant
fingers with stubby strength—
my first boyfriend held this brown
hand and called me "milkmaid."

My father's hands were blunt, too,
broader than the piano keys.
Time ticks on. Artist "Grandma"
Layton drew hands by contour
with all the lines and blemishes
etched without vanity. Praying hands
like steeples, and healing hands.
A pulse also ticks at the wrist.

Time is in the dough rising
after the kneading and waiting,
and in the choir director's hands
that slow the bass and lift the soprano.
We try to understand time
and can only say it is in God's hands.

ELIZABETH SCHULTZ

MRS. NOAH TAKES THE HELM

We set no sails. We climbed no rigging.
We moved according to the waves' whim,
the wind's will, the moon's fancy.
Across that vast plain of water, we bobbed
and bounced, little more than sea foam
as uncertain and hopeful as milkweed fluff.
Only Noah noted our direction. The sun's
rise and fall gave us east and west, and he
fixed the ark's bow on a point in between.
Only Noah kept time. On the long pine
that was our tiller, he marked the days.

At night, we lost both time and direction.
Shade came over us like a familiar tent,
the stars shining through its worn canvas.
Noah slept among the goats and sheep,
and I stood watch while the ark surged
into darkness. On certain nights, I nudged
the tiller and took us out onto the moon's path.
Phosphorescence flickered in the water.
The eyes of ocelots, and lemurs, and owls
glowed. For company I had the sibilance
of chimpanzees snoring and a coyote
duet ricocheting off the invisible horizon.
No one would tell when I guided the ark
skyward, up onto the highway of stars
to meet Draco, and Pegasus, and Aquila,
and all our glittering ancestors.

MRS. NOAH BREATHES WITH THE ANIMALS

I was exhausted
by miracles, the sea spewing
flames, islands heaved up
before my eyes, swirling stars.
My knuckles were scrubbed
raw with saltwater, my ankles
plushly swollen. The animals
were all mouths, gaping,
snoring, tongues spit-slathered.
Only Noah remained upright,
a reed, stiffened in the wind.
I fed them all indifferently.
There was no seventh day to rest.
Everyone had stopped counting.

I left slop for the tigers,
their yellow eyes burning
bright rings on my back.
There was fish enough for
the bears, but their dark eyes
rolled and searched mine
with questions beyond Why.
The pigs' slimy snouts nudged
my hands. The cows' damp
noses pressed into my breast.
Perhaps the kangaroo, dainty

hands lifted to her face, prayed.
There were no answers, only
the surge of our breathing.

ELIZABETH SCHULTZ

MRS. NOAH AMIDST THE BIRDS

Frigate birds circled overhead,
orienting us to the turning sky.
Our claustrophobic fowls gawked
to see such free-wheeling. Crated
on deck, they took the spray.
The peacock, palsied with salt,
paled, and the turkey shriveled.

All that time we drifted aimlessly,
the long-winged albatross observed
our position. Out of the empty sky,
she came calling to perch among
our phantoms, preening and posturing
in the serenity of her freedom.
She'd flown over islands yesterday,
would head for shaley shores tomorrow.
I, too, was crated, my span limited to
this man, these gunwales, this horizon,
and out of spite, I wished the albatross
dead from a madman's crossbow and
nets as endless as the seas she traced.

Desperate for variety, I set the raven free.
Like soot, he dissolved into mist. We waited.
When he did not return, I was glad
for this one bird. A narcissist, he would
survive without us. I chose his opposite
to send out next. Pliant and plump, the dove
would not follow the albatross' high course.

116

She vanished into light drizzle. We waited.
When she returned and flew through
the rainbow's arch, I gave up spite, and
opening all our cages, sang with the fowls.

JESSIE BROWN

WHAT WE DON'T KNOW WE KNOW

Systole, diastole. The strength of soft tunnels
opening and closing. The shifting
color of blood, the delicate gases
that trigger the next breath.

When to drink; when to release
the salt of sweat, or tears.
How to read the image reversed
on the dark inside of the retina.

Where the stars come from, behind
closed lids. How the marrow builds.
What kind of work makes a callus.
How to scab over a wound.

When to grow old. Where to line
the skin's tired creases. Why a body,
plunging under, wants to surface again.
When to stop loving, after the loved one has gone.

JESSIE BROWN

GRAPEFRUIT

Don't be sorry, ma'am, be grateful,
was what the ragged man said
when I breathed Sorry and kept walking
as he stood on the corner for spare change.
He was bearded, wrapped
in blankets, night and rain.

That was the fall. But it comes back
like a tide, with ordinary things—
This sun. Shoes. A spoonful
of red grapefruit, out of season.
One more thing to give thanks for,
the sweetness and the sting of it,
even as the sweetness slides on down.

CHRIS R. E. WELLS

MOONLIGHT

It chanced we stood
amid the superstition,
the moonlight of small hours
spoiled by saws.

      Before I reached despair, some fresh talaria delivered a smile from John, whose feet married the soil, begetting posterity of prints upon the world. He still had faith in a rainbow obscured by night.

This was not my confidence.
So many soon were dead.
This was quickly a killed land.

CHRIS R. E. WELLS

GHOSTS

On the warm shore I frequently sat
and pondered the ghosts.
They were apparently charmed.
They hovered around me and
danced in their way
to this ribbed tune

strewn over with dark hissing.

I had formerly come to see these pines adventurously, as skyrockets to air, to make my own thread among the gentle worms. At the edge of the water I often hung to a fire and, when done, without companion I would throw the burning nights high and watch them softly descend.

They said
when we reached the bottom
we would all be whistling.
Then they took the moon.

Soon everything in the forest was quenched. We were suddenly groping in total wrecks.

CHRIS R. E. WELLS

WOODCHOPPERS

So many fat chimneys are now in that great vale. The smoke is the grandchild of the pines. I wonder who in the horizon still hides from the city fires.

Long ago
I went over
some bare camp
where woodchoppers
left their kindlings.
We are natural after all. So let us live.

Old snow, at least, will still be found
atop their sheds in March
though the forest all
around them became
shadows of houses

(with the occasional leaf
blemishing bare
ground).

CHRIS R. E. WELLS

MEMORY

I was brought from potato vines through this
my native corn blades.
I have comes through these bean leaves
to this influence, this presence.
It is one of the oldest daguerreotypes
developed on my memory.
These landscapes, these pastures, these skyscrapers
are all walked over tonight.

I have cooked my old eyes in the aspect
of fallen johnswort.
A new growth is rising, preparing
other stumps all around.
Almost the same pines echo and spring
from the same perennial waters.
I have at length paved the fabulous
streets of my infant
memory.

In this town,
this city I see the pond
in the wood and the field,

the oldest scenes.

PETRA MCQUEEN

NOW HE HAS LEFT

Now he has left, the door safely shut,
The house breathes a sigh:
Settles, exhales; joints creak relief.
Taps drip, then stop. Dust falls and lies.

She sits on the sofa and is still.
Silence settles like a gift.
Thoughts drift and are dispersed
She breathes gently: fall and lift.

Upstairs, her daughter slumbers.
Empty of dreams, darkness weaves
A blanket of rest to cover her limbs.
Her breath is deep, her chest heaves.

And yes, the morning must come,
And light will crack a crisp new dawn
And the sun will rise on a different day,
But now, they breathe behind a closed door.

PAULA LIPPARD JUSTICE

MARY'S BREASTS

for Rebecca

Imagine Mary's breasts,
warm brown as the earth
pale gold as the moon,
the breasts of a young girl
ripe as perfect plums.

Imagine the angel who came to her—blinding!
How beneath her breasts her heart opened like a mouth
to receive the host,
how her belly nest-like
encircled the seed.

Imagine how she labored
and how they lay, wet and spent,
against each other's skin,
how mouth and tiny hands reached for the milk taut breasts
for the sweet purpled nipple.

Imagine how in all the years that followed,
there in the pocket of her heart
she knew what was to come.
See her before the cross,
how her breast split open like the sky
and left a wound where her heart had been.

Imagine Mary's breasts
how they are like your own.
How beneath them your heart
must open to receive the terrible gift of love,
how you must nurture the child within your own darkness
bringing forth in travail.
See how you must feed the least
with milk of kindness.
Imagine in the end
how your breast will be rent,
how love's wound will consume you.

BRYAN R. MONTE

GLASGOW MEETING

The warden asks if I'd "rather take the lift."
"Next time" I say as I lean into the wooden rail
Of the converted mid-town mansion's
Grand brown and white winding staircase.
Once upstairs in the meeting room
I sit down a bit too heavily, wheezing
Into one of the many empty chairs
That fill up as meeting gathers.

I close my eyes and think
Of Friday's Lake Windermere cruise
Saturday's whitewashed Dove Cottage
And listen to the rainy, river rush
Of traffic on the elevated M8
A block away, trying to forget
The burning in my right leg
The ringing in my ears
A week of 2 AM hotel
Corridor shouts and door slams
And think of the strangers
Next to me who are Friends
As I center down and listen.

I sit and quietly count my breaths
Cleaning up the messy house
That is my mind and body
From the damp, musty basement
To the cluttered, dusty attic
Until I feel the warm morning sun

127

Shine through the tall windows
Brightening against my closed eyelids
Light, light, more light
LIGHT, LIGHT, MORE LIGHT
My leg no longer burning
My ears no longer ringing
Seventy men, women and children
Sitting in silence in the upper room.

BRYAN R. MONTE

THE BOATS

I.

I rest my head on the rounded coolness of your stomach
And stretch out cupped in your long arms and legs
As if you were a boat
And sleep a journey downstream.

II.

Warm water and soap
Edible ivory skin
I suck the water out of your hair
Stroke foamy chrysanthemums on your back
You buckle beneath the showerhead waterfall
Your big hands frothing.

III.

Tell me I'm not walking into another river
Choking on the shiny grey sweat
Of freshly shaven faces and airless lips
Slipping down past unoffered muscular arms
I hear my loves singing to their loves in boats overhead
Sitting on the green bottom loam
Fish caress me with unblinking eyes.

ALL ROADS

In Memoriam, Ron Linder

All roads lead to the same place
We said laughing to each other
Listening to John Cage on the car radio
That Presidents' Day weekend, unbelievers
Lost in the sudden, spring-green, Olema Hills
Looking for the Vedanta retreat
The day after we heard the bald, brown
Orange-robed swami chant
OM—Shanti, Shanti, Shanti
OM—Shanti, Shanti, Shanti
In his peach socks and brown wingtips
And say: *The teacher is the student,*
       and the student, the teacher
And suddenly we exchanged places
Fathers and sons to one another
My arms swelling strangely from your tetanus shot
My ex-lover barricaded in the back bedroom
Coughing through Christmas with pneumocystis
As we read poems at my kitchen table
About lunch counter dinners and interstate abductions
Your mother's monthly suicide threats
Or the iron block in the front door lock
Your father reamed with a $20 bill
Until your family disappeared in the middle of the night
Your brother laughing at the landlord
Your parti-colored books left behind
On the shelf over the radiator.

The years we gave to those who never loved us
The years we lost to those who never knew us
Borrowing money for textbooks, going without meals
Sleeping on the sofa or the floor
Working weekends, school breaks, summer vacations
Watching the smiling, tanned college men with their dates
Rush out of the stadium after the game
As we rode the bus home from another Saturday shift
Arms still twitching from typing contracts or mopping floors
To pay the tuition, to earn the diploma, to get permission
To make the endless daily rounds with maddening precision
From nursing home to hospital to office
From insurance office to night school to students' homes
The 9:30 PM private English lessons
The 3 AM hospital admissions
The booze, the drugs, the invisible armies
Under the skin that carried our friends away
The paperwork glaciers that froze out our poetry
Then buried, ground up, and wore away the years
Cannot be undone no matter how carefully we turn
On these steep, green hills above the Pacific Ocean
Breaking beneath us or ask the swami for directions
OM—Shanti, Shanti, Shanti
OM—Shanti, Shanti, Shanti
He chants as we sit and wait to go home.

BRYAN R. MONTE

ONE CANVAS

Archaeology is not for the living
But those obsessed with the past
Conned by the old maxim
Forgetfulness dooming repetition
Or psychotherapy's promise
That remembrance brings release

Sometimes forgetfulness is a gift
If it stops the daydreams or midnight visits
To the shrines of our private failures:
The cardboard boxes of photographs and letters
The abandoned art school projects
The faded scout uniform or yellowed wedding dress
Jammed into closets or stacked up in the attic
The wind whispering against the roof
Your mind going four different directions
As you struggle to fall asleep.

A balanced life requires economy
To move ahead with what we can bare
Or scan and store on a computer drive
Which never grows heavier.
Buried under our own debris
There is no space for living
Art is the careful choice of what to keep
Like Titian's ghost men
Painted over as the master
Worked out his composition
Subtraction as addition.

132

Repaint your life on one canvas
No need to mention
What it took to get there.

THE RED SONNET

Struck skin flushes hot with a florid sting,
But the welt proclaims the slap is over.
Bloodshot eyes hint of a sweet night lover
With fast beating hearts, sated skin glowing.

Cherry, roon, vermilion, ruby, seeping
Blood shared in a pact with another.
Locked hands as children shout red rover
With breathless wonder youthful games bring.

Worn out words fail the singers who will say
You are like a fresh rose laden with dew
And blaze like sunset on a sanguine day.
Poets write old words in verse by the slew
But you will frustrate a simple cliché.
My Titian haired love, pain ends with you.

KAREN HEAD

MY PARIS YEAR TROIS

under the influence of Frank O'Hara and Mina Loy

Bruce Willis held the door for me at *Chanel*
a story that should stand on its own merits
or lack thereof, except that later, at dinner,
after I regale everyone with my "famous person" story
Martina begins to discuss the beauty
of *Notre Dame*, the church not the woman,
except it really is about the woman
because what we are questioning
is spirituality itself, and I say,
Even a self-professed atheist should be moved,
but Andrew hears, *Even a sock-wearing atheist,*
and we laugh, except there is an air of something
unsaid, something perhaps about what it means
to be moved, so Jay and Maria make a joke
about *coq au vin* always sounding pornographic,
which we all agree, not being French,
is appropriately French, except *coq* is cock
in our language, the American sound being
a large part of what seems illicit, which isn't
the same as explicit, something we are all
trying to be, but failing to do,
particularly exceptional when you consider
that words are our vocation—
if this were one century earlier,
the men would escort us to our hotel
leave us alone with our prayers
head for *Montmartre's Cabaret du Néant*
hold the door open for sin—

135

instead, I order another round of Kir,
thrust my right pinky into the candle flame,
shake loose my hair, find any temptation
entirely my own.

JOHN GILHAM

OF COURSE, IT GOES ON,

Even in bombed cities people need bread;
the peach crop, spared by the night's bombardment
must still be sold, or rot;
and the butchers killed their meat yesterday;
life goes on.

The market buys and sells, though the soldiers
dart from cover to cover a block away.
and each morning, after the blitz,
we stepped over hosepipes to our offices.

Where the twin shadow fell but yesterday
the coffee shop re-opens.

For this is the affirmation:
this is how we say
that you who love war
cannot destroy us.

The bombed grocer who is "more open than usual";
those who make love in the shelter;
the girl going to school past the burned out tank;
the mother who sings her child to sleep
through the stutter of gunfire, with songs
that are centuries old—of course, it goes on.

Out of the rubble we crawl with our violins,
our scraps of poetry, our cooking pots

and shopping bags; starting now
to rebuild what makes us human,
defying the teeth, the wolves of war.

JOHN GILHAM

GETTING THERE

After Köln, where the smell of cabbage drifted across the station,
we sped south, threading the tidy streets of Bonn
like an intrusion on a maiden aunt, until suddenly
vineyards appeared, knitted up the hillsides,
ribbed experiments in colour choice,
folded to let a castle (ruin, museum, smart hotel) adorn a rock,
while on the Rhine, dashed with white like a mountain stream,
Europe's barges battered the waves.

Later, from a high apartment, we watch as darkness falls:
lights move and sway as if we are still voyaging—
an inland sea, a Brio set, crossing and recrossing the fields
with bright skeins of earnest travellers,
patterns in light, a country on the move.

And we move too, on clockwork trains,
past peaceful woods, fields of dry corn, and bare orchards.
We visit quiet towns, cafés with cakes you might die for,
or from; sausages and sauerkraut, paving, baroque altars,
and litter pre-sorted, purposeful, neat.

We drive, we visit friends, we see the sights;
but in one place, on a farm wagon, a tarpaulin
and a name—Mengele—angel of death,
strikes like a shard of ice impaling the heart.
I think "farm machinery firm"—in vain.
Here lies the poison of history:

it chills these golden hills;
it lurks behind the smiles.

We cannot avoid what we inherit—
but we must know it for what it is and how it shapes us.

The town to which we return, have dinner
with friends who live there,
in '45 was rubble on the map.

JOHN GILHAM

THE OLD GATE AT WITTENBURG

The players were the first to go,
hung over, tattered, with their wagons and stuff,
pursued by urchins and unpaid innkeepers,
heading north to towns and palaces heard of
from student princes, late, after the show,
everyone drunk and maudlin, nostalgic,
promising the perfect audience back home.

And next him, heir apparent, in black already,
posting north in pride and fear,
launched by his father's death from student prince to king
in the time it takes to break a seal.

And his friend, puzzled,
borne on some dark rumor of foul play,
of wars and weddings, danger and death,
loyalty, curiosity, a kind of love.

And last, the two sent for, paid to go,
knowing who called the tune, the shots,
employed to build enquiry upon acquaintance,
hired men on hired mounts.

And of all these, only one returned,
passed the gate and rode slowly
back to his lodgings. He was heard to say
that now Philosophy held no terrors—
he had been to the end of heaven and earth,
had seen there all that he would ever know.

JAMES HANNON

IN PRAISE OF DANGEROUS WOMEN

Long raven hair like Spanish moss
grabs a runaway slave
in a Louisiana swamp—
bound fast to the mast
for his siren song,
like a horn through the fog
of the bayou bog
where Morgan Le Fay rises again
from the mist of his boyhood dreams.

Somehow he pulls free but his head is shorn—
like a nameless prison inmate
or a tonsured monk reborn
with a safer, and holy name.
In the numinous light of the piney woods,
nel mezzo del cammin (as he understood)
he follows the trail, like a well-bred hound,
of the sanguinous scent
drifting toward the ground.

When he gets to the crossroads
he tosses his bones.
To no one's surprise
those single point dice
stare up at him like the Siamese eyes
that called him out with a smoky smile—
she said, "some go that way and some go this."
He tastes her again when he bites his lip.

He had laughed years before
at a bright-eyed young man
who had pulled his coat
with a trembling hand
and spilled out a story
of the horrible toll
of the triple Scorpio
who stole his soul.

The broken man had sighed
and let his calling card reply—
Blake's etching of hell
and an experienced verse:
the road of excess
(may first make things worse
but it) leads to the palace of wisdom.

Stare at the sun.
Stare at a woman
who knows what she's done
and hasn't a single regret.

Reach behind you
for something to throw
through those black mirrored eyes.
Hear the blood rush in your ears.
Feel your feet tingle.
Feel your arms shake.
Scream 'til the rafters
threaten to break.

Breathe.

Breathe again.
Open your hands.

Laugh at yourself.
Begin.

JAMES HANNON

WINTER BIRDS

It was the year I quit coffee,
five years after booze
and four years after cigarettes.

I shoveled the whole driveway
in a January blizzard
and my middle-aged, momentarily
caffeine-free heart
made not a murmur of protest.
I felt like a righteous Mormon,
Brigham Young on the edge of the desert.
I wanted to go back in the house
and make another baby with you.
But it was past time for that.

Susanna bundled out to help
plowing though snow almost to her waist.
We heard crows complaining overhead
as they always do in snow.
A bluejay hopped by, ignoring us,
and chickadees screamed
at the feeder across the street.

It suddenly struck her,
"Haven't they gone south yet?"
I told her that some stay all year.
She finished a path
with her bright red shovel
and went inside.

In a minute I felt tired
and wanted a smoke.
I watched the snowfall slow
and collect on my glasses.

I caught for a moment that smell
of wet childhood winters,
stamped my boots
and started on the cars.

JOHN WOOLMAN

based on text from his journal

Love was the first motion, this white stone
the opening spring of living waters
from the silence, at no time seeking for words,
laboring for an inward stillness,

uttering that which truth opened,
sometimes in much weakness,
standing like a trumpet,
the room full and the people quiet.

His word was in my heart
a burning fire shut in my bones;
weary with forbearing
I could not stay.

Lying in the wilderness looking
at the stars, slavery appeared to me
as a dark gloominess hanging over the land,
the murmurs of oppression.

Meditating on lands sold for trifles,
the wild beasts not so plentiful
skins and furs wasted on liquor,
my heart enlarged in pure love.

I took ship. The sea wrought exceedingly,
and the high, foaming waves appeared like fire,

147

the poor bewildered sailors
full of corruption and alienation.

I traveled northwards, finding peace in labor,
found the price of mutton, wheat and rye,
wood for fire very scarce and dear.
United with the suffering seed

a love clothes my mind while I write
of the peaceable kingdom
from sea to sea, and from the river
to the ends of the earth.

Let us rest ourselves in the rock
which shakings shall not move.
I hope I shall shortly go to rest.
John Woolman is dead. Dwell deep.

NOTES ON CONTRIBUTORS

MICHAEL BROEK's chapbook *The Logic of Yoo* was issued by *Beloit Poetry Journal* in 2011, and his poems have appeared or are forthcoming in *The Literary Review*, *Blackbird*, *From the Fishouse*, *The American Poetry Review*, *Literary Imagination*, and elsewhere in print and online. He is the recipient of a scholarship to the Bread Loaf Writers Conference, a New Jersey State Poetry Fellowship from the New Jersey State Arts Council, and he is the Managing Editor of *Mead: The Magazine of Literature and Libations*.

JESSIE BROWN leads poetry programs in schools, libraries and community centers in the Boston area. She's published two short collections, *Lucky*, the 2011 Anabiosis Press Chapbook winner, and *What We Don't Know We Know*, from Finishing Line Press. A founding member of the Alewife Poets, she gives performances and workshops both in collaboration and alone. She has an M.A. from Stanford and lives in Arlington, Massachusetts.

JENNY DOUGHTY is originally British but has lived in Maine since 2002. She is a former English teacher, and Education Adviser to Penguin Books in the UK. In the United States, her poems have been featured in *Gestalt Review*, *Horticulture* magazine, *Pulse* online review, *Naugatuck River Review*, and *Four Way Review*. She is a member of Portland Friends Meeting.

ANDREA ENGLAND is a mother and a doctoral student at Western Michigan University. Her poems have appeared or are forthcoming in *Passages North*, *DMQ Review*, *Cutthroat Magazine*, *RHINO*, and other journals. She lives in Kalamazoo, Michigan.

JOHN GILHAM lives in York, England, where he recently retired from a career in social housing. His first poetry collection, *Fosdyke and Me and Other Poems*, appeared in 2010 and he has also been published in numerous magazines in the UK. He is a member of York (Friargate) Quaker Meeting.

JAMES HANNON is a psychotherapist in Massachusetts where he accompanies adolescents and adults recovering from depression, disappointment and addiction, and looking for a life of meaning and joy. He is a member of Cambridge Friends Meeting. His poems have appeared recently or are forthcoming in *Assisi*, *Blue Lake Review*, *Time of Singing*, *Victorian Violet Press*, and *The Wayfarer*.

HEIDI HART is a singer, a Pushcart Prize-winning poet, and the author of the memoir *Grace Notes*. She holds an M.F.A. in creative writing from Sarah Lawrence College and is currently working toward a doctorate in German Studies at Duke, where she researches literature and music in the context of war. This past summer she taught a creative writing course in Berlin.

KAREN HEAD is the author of *Sassing* (WordTech, 2009), *My Paris Year* (All Nations, 2009) and *Shadow Boxes* (All Nations, 2003). Also a digital poet, her collaborative exquisite corpse "Monumental" was created via Twitter while she stood atop the Fourth Plinth in Trafalgar Square as part of Antony Gormley's One and Other Project, and was detailed in a *TIME* online mini-documentary. She teaches at Georgia Tech.

ERROL HESS is the founding editor of *The Sow's Ear Poetry Review*. His writing has appeared in publications including *Poets & Writers, Friends Journal, Blue Fifth Review*, and was anthologized in the books *Writers at the Fork* and *Homework*. He lives near Due West, South Carolina, and currently clerks Southern Appalachian Yearly Meeting's Ministry and Nurture committee.

PHYLLIS HOGE [formerly Thompson] taught poetry and world literature for many years at the University of Hawai'i, where she also initiated in 1966 the first Poets in the Schools program in America, raised her four children, and published five books of poetry before retiring to Albuquerque. Her most recent collection, *HELLO, HOUSE,* celebrates domestic tasks, each poem illustrated by Maxine Hong Kingston.

ADAM HOULE lives in Lubbock, Texas. His poems have appeared in *AGNI, Blackbird,* and *Willow Springs,* as well as the anthologies *Best New Poets 2010, Dogs Singing,* and *Improbable Worlds.* He is a Ph.D. candidate at Texas Tech University.

NATHANIEL HUNT lives in Boston, Massachusetts, where he is working toward his M.F.A. at UMass-Boston. He also works as a freelance writer, editor, and tutor. His poems have been featured in *Iconoclast, The Houston Literary Review, Poetry Quarterly,* and *Pennsylvania Literary Journal,* among others.

EILEEN R. KINCH studied writing as ministry at Earlham School of Religion. A writer and editor, she lives in Lancaster County, Pennsylvania. She is a member of Keystone Friends Meeting.

GEOFFREY KNOWLTON was raised in the Hannover, New Hampshire Friends Meeting and was a pastor in the United Church of Christ for many years before returning to his Quaker roots. He is a member of the Worcester, Massachusetts Meeting. Geoff is a psychotherapist and writes poetry, usually sonnets, whenever he finds a moment to scribble notes.

DUSTIN JUNKERT lives in Portland, Oregon. He recently won a *New York Times* essay contest and has published poetry in *The Journal, South Carolina Review, the minnesota review, Georgetown Review, Grey Sparrow,* and *Euphony.*

PAULA LIPPARD JUSTICE is a retired undergraduate and graduate faculty member and currently an Associate Adjunct Professor in Counseling and Communication at Old Dominion University in Norfolk, Virginia. Dr. Justice is also a Recorded Minister in the Religious Society of Friends (Quakers) and has been a member of the Virginia Beach Friends Meeting since 1973.

Though JENNIFER LUEBBERS was born and raised in the Roman Catholic faith, she has in adulthood come to find a spiritual home in the Quaker tradition. She currently serves as Editor of *Indiana Review* at Indiana University, where she is an M.F.A. candidate. Her work has appeared or is forthcoming in *Crab Orchard Review*, *Massachusetts Review*, *Ninth Letter*, and *Washington Square Review*, among others.

LAURA MCCULLOUGH is the author of four poetry collections, including *Rigger Death & Hoist Another* (Black Lawrence Press) and *Panic* (Alice James Books), and the editor of *The Room & the World: Essays on Stephen Dunn* (Syracuse University Press) and *Essays on Poetry and Race: The Task of Un/Masking* (University of Georgia Press). She is the editor of *Mead: The Magazine of Literature and Libations* and an editor at large for *TranStudies Magazine*.

MIKE MCGEEHON works, plays, and lives in Newberg, Oregon. He has worked as a social worker, a janitor, a nursing home attendant, and for the last eight years, as a public school teacher.

PETRA MCQUEEN is a writer and creative writing teacher. She's also written e-biographies of Shakespeare and Dickens. Petra is kept busy and entertained by her two lovely boys.

MARIA MELENDEZ is author of two poetry collections from University of Arizona Press: *Flexible Bones*, a Colorado Book Award Finalist, and *How Long She'll Last in This World*, a finalist for the PEN Center USA Literary Award. Her work appears in *Orion* magazine and other venues. A former clerk of the board of *Western Friend* magazine, she is a member of Logan Monthly Meeting in Utah and attends Colorado Springs Monthly Meeting.

ROSALIE MOFFETT was the winner of a 2012 Discovery/*Boston Review* poetry prize. Her work has appeared or is forthcoming in *The Believer*, *Field*, *Hayden's Ferry Review*, *The Normal School*, *32 Poems*, and elsewhere. She is a Washington native currently living in Indiana.

BRYAN R. MONTE is a writer and instructor who publishes and edits *Amsterdam Quarterly*, a tri-quarterly, online, English-language literary journal. His poetry has appeared in *Bay Windows*, *Irreantum*, *Sunstone*, and *Friends Journal*. He has lived in the Netherlands for twenty years and is a member of Amsterdam Monthly Meeting.

ESTHER GREENLEAF MURER is a member of Central Philadelphia Monthly Meeting. She was founding editor of *Types & Shadows*, the journal of the Fellowship of Quakers in the Arts, and edited *Beyond Uneasy Tolerance*, a historical compilation of Quaker quotations on the arts. She published her first poetry collection, *Unglobed Fruit*, in 2011. Her poems have appeared in *Friends Journal* and in numerous literary magazines, mostly online. She was featured poet in the February 2011 issue of *The Centrifugal Eye*.

AARON J. POLLER was born in the Bronx in 1947. He has worked in mental health nursing since the early 1970s and currently works as a nurse psychotherapist. His poems have appeared in numerous magazines and journals. He is a member of Salem Creek Friends and lives in Winston-Salem, North Carolina.

DAWN POTTER directs the Frost Place Conference on Poetry and Teaching, held each summer at Robert Frost's home in Franconia, New Hampshire. Her most recent book is an anthology, *A Poet's Sourcebook: Writings about Poetry from the Ancient World to the Present* (Autumn House Press, 2013). She lives in Harmony, Maine.

JANICE MILLER POTTER is the author of two poetry books, *Meanwell* and *Psalms in Time*. Her poetry has appeared in *Poet Lore*, *Connecticut Review*, *Worcester Review*, *Adirondack Review*, *Christian Science Monitor*, *The Sow's Ear Poetry Review*, *Pittsburgh Quarterly*, and elsewhere. Winner of the 2005 Sara Henderson Hay Poetry Prize, she has taught at Rhode Island College. She lives in Cornwall, Vermont.

DAVID RAY is the author of 23 books, including *Hemingway: A Desperate Life* (Whirlybird Press), *When* (Howling Dog Press), and *Music of Time: Selected & New Poems* (Backwaters Press). *The Endless Search* (Soft Skull Press) is his memoir. David co-founded *American Writers Against the Vietnam War*, and his activism continues to challenge. An emeritus professor of the University of Missouri-Kansas City, he was founding editor of *New Letters* and, with Judy Ray, *New Letters On The Air*.

JUDY RAY, poet and essayist, grew up in Sussex, England, and has lived in many other parts of the world. Now, with her poet husband, David, she makes her home in Tucson, Arizona, where she is a member of Pima Monthly Meeting. Her latest poetry book is *To Fly Without Wings*.

ANN RITTER, in addition to having journalism credits, has received an artist-initiated grant in writing from the Georgia Council for the Arts. She has published fiction, essays and poetry in *Charleston Magazine*, *Confrontation*, *GSU Review*, *Earth's Daughters*, *THEMA*, and *Georgia Journal*. Her work has been previously anthologized in *Like a Summer Peach: Sunbright Poems & Old Southern Recipes* and *The Southern Poetry Anthology, Volume V: Georgia*.

AIRLIE SATTLER ROSE is a member of Durham Friends Meeting (NCYM-C). Her life has taken her from a doctoral program in Zoology at Duke to an M.F.A. in poetry at UTPA. Currently, she works as an Assistant Director of the UMass-Amherst Writing Center while studying composition and rhetoric. At home, she enjoys the creative energy of her family, garden, and community.

LAUREN RUSK teaches at Stanford University and spends summers in Oxford, England. Her books include *Pictures in the Firestorm: Poems* and *The Life Writing of Otherness: Woolf, Baldwin, Kingston, and Winterson*. Her recent work has appeared in *Best New Poets*, *Hotel Amerika*, *The Writer's Chronicle*, and the anthology *Come Together: Imagine Peace*.

SIBYL RUTH lives in Birmingham, England and is a member of Central England Area Meeting. She has published two collections of poetry: *Nothing Personal* (Iron Press, 1995) and *I Could Become That Woman* (Five Leaves, 2003). She scripted and presented a documentary on Quaker poetry, *Listen to Them Breathing*, for BBC Radio 4.

SARAH SARAI's collection, *The Future Is Happy* (BlazeVOX), was published in 2009. Her poems are in *Boston Review*, *Threepenny Review*, *Gargoyle* and other journals, and in anthologies including *Say It Loud: Poems About James Brown* (Whirlwind Press) and

157

Maintenant (Three Rooms Press). She has an M.F.A. in fiction from Sarah Lawrence College and is contributing editor at *The Writing Disorder*.

ELIZABETH SCHULTZ, having retired from the University of Kansas in 2001, now balances scholarship on Herman Melville and on the environment with writing essays and poems about the people and places she loves. In addition to two critical works on Melville, two collections of poetry, a book of short stories, and a book of nature essays, her scholarly essays and poetry have been published widely.

MARIAN KAPLUN SHAPIRO, a psychologist, and member of Cambridge Friends Meeting, is the author of a professional book, *Second Childhood*, and three poetry books: *Players in the Dream, Dreamers in the Play*; *Your Third Wish*; and *The End of the World, Announced on Wednesday*. Four-time Senior Poet Laureate of Massachusetts, she was nominated for the Pushcart Prize in 2012.

MARYHELEN SNYDER is a Quaker, psychotherapist, and writer, currently living in Virginia after forty years in New Mexico. She has authored a memoir in prose and poetry entitled *No Hole in the Flame*. She has published widely in literary journals, and her essays on poetry have appeared in *Poet Lore* and *Rattle*. Her most recent book of poetry is *Sun in an Empty Room*, available from Amazon.

MARGARET STETLER's poems have appeared in *Pearl, Kosmos, The West Wind Review*, and other literary magazines. Her collection *Woman of Myriad Seeds* is soon to be published. A refugee from post-9/11 New York City, she now lives in Winchester, Virginia, with her husband and four cats where she teaches a creativity workshop, substitutes in the city's schools, and attends Hopewell Centre Meeting.

EMILY MAE STOKES' work has been featured in *Collision Literary Magazine*, *The Dirty Napkin*, *Stone Highway Review*, *PANK*, and *The Monongahela Review*. Her first manuscript, *What Happens in the End*, was featured as a short collection in *Embark* (Toadlily Press, 2012). Stokes was recently nominated for a Pushcart Prize and is currently pursuing an M.F.A. degree at Sarah Lawrence College.

KEJT WALSH is a sometime student, long-time social justice activist, and full-time human living in Eugene, Oregon. Kejt grew up in Des Moines, Iowa, and has been Quaker since attending a summer camp at Earlham College in high school. Kejt's poetry can be found in places like *Architrave Press*, *Bluestem*, and *PANK*.

ELLEN WEHLE has had poems appear in journals such as *Slate*, *The New England Review*, *Poetry Daily*, *The New Republic*, *Notre Dame Review*, *The Southern Review*, and *Colorado Review*. Her book, *The Ocean Liner's Wake*, came out from Shearsman in 2009. She lives outside Philadelphia, where she is completing her first novel.

RICHARD MARX WEINRAUB taught at the University of Puerto Rico for twenty-three years. He has published two collections of poetry: *Wonder Bread Hill* and *Heavenly Bodies*; a third entitled *Lapidary* will be published in 2013. His work has appeared in *The Paris Review*, *Asheville Poetry Review*, *South Carolina Review*, *The Hampden-Sydney Poetry Review*, *Green Mountains Review*, *North American Review*, *Slate*, and *River Styx*.

CHRIS R. E. WELLS lives in Ohio. Flaming Giblet Press, Teeny Tiny Publications, and Sacrifice Press and have published his work, which has also appeared in several online journals. He was co-editor of the now defunct journal *21 Stars Review*, the complete works of which are archived at Sundress Publications.

MARTIN WILLITTS, JR. is a retired Senior Librarian living in Syracuse, New York. His forthcoming poetry books include *Waiting for the Day to Open Its Wings* (UNBOUND Content), *Art Is the Impression of an Artist* (Edgar and Lenore's Publishing House), *Swimming in the Ladle of Stars* (Kattywompus Press), and *Searching for What Is Not There* (Hiraeth Press).

PAMELA MURRAY WINTERS' poems have appeared in *Gettysburg Review*, *Gargoyle*, *JMWW*, *Fledgling Rag*, *Delmarva Poetry Review*, *Innisfree Poetry Journal*, the anthology *Takoma Park Writers 1981*, and other publications. She lives in Silver Spring, Maryland.

KRISTIN CAMITTA ZIMET is the editor of *The Sow's Ear Poetry Review*, a journal of fine poetry and fine art. She is the author of *Take in My Arms the Dark*, a full-length poetry collection. Her poems are in journals including *Salt Hill*, *Crab Orchard Review*, and *Poet Lore*. She is a member of Hopewell Centre Friends Meeting.

REPRINT CREDITS

Ron Waddams (1920–2010): "Publishers of Truth" (cover art). Reprinted by permission of the Larren Art Trust; Ian McFarlane, clerk.

Jessie Brown: "Grapefruit," *Peaceworks*. "What We Don't Know We Know," *Comstock Review* and *What We Don't Know We Know* (Finishing Line Press). Reprinted by permission of the author.

John Gilham: "Of Course It Goes On," *Acumen Literary Journal* and *Fosdyke and Me and Other Poems* (Fighting Cock Press). "The Old Gate at Wittenburg," *Acumen Literary Journal* and *Fosdyke and Me and Other Poems*. "Getting There," *Fosdyke and Me and Other Poems*. Reprinted by permission of the author.

James Hannon: "Winter Birds," *Soundings East* and *Chantarelle's Notebook*. Reprinted by permission of the author.

Karen Head: "My Paris Year Trois," *My Paris Year* (All Nations Press). Reprinted by permission of the author.

Errol Hess: "Bird Shadows," *Blue Fifth Review*. "Unbuilding," *Madison Review*. Reprinted by permission of the author.

Phyllis Hoge: "The Light on the Door," *Hudson Review*. "Two Photographs," *Hudson Review*. "What We Give," *Comstock Review*. Reprinted by permission of the author.

Adam Houle: "We'd Learn Later Her Husband Left," *Cave Wall*. "Chihuahua Nativity Scene," *DIAGRAM*. "Somniloquence on the High Plains," *Roanoke Review*. Reprinted by permission of the author.

Nathaniel Hunt: "St. Johns, Oregon, Soon After My Grandfather's Death," *Paper Nautilus*. Reprinted by permission of the author.

Eileen R. Kinch: "Fermentation," *Enlivened by the Mystery: Quakers and God* (Friends Bulletin Corporation). Reprinted by permission of the author.

Jennifer Luebbers: "Barn Elegy," *Washington Square*. "Petitions," *Ninth Letter*. Reprinted by permission of the author.

Laura McCullough: "Holy," *Birmingham Poetry Review*. Reprinted by permission of the author.

Maria Melendez: "Behind Every Good Soldier," *Flexible Bones* (University of Arizona Press). "To Hope," *Flexible Bones*. "Love Song for a War God," *Flexible Bones*. "A Different Sympathy," *How Long She'll Last in This World* (University of Arizona Press). "An Argument for the Brilliance of All Things," *How Long She'll Last in This World*. "Good News for Humans," *How Long She'll Last in This World*. Reprinted by permission of the author.

Rosalie Moffett: "Sunday Evening Meeting for Worship at 1435 Columbia St. Apt. 2," *32 Poems*. "Instar and Eclose," *32 Poems*. "Knecht w/ Nature," *Boston Review*. Reprinted by permission of the author.

Bryan R. Monte: "The Boats," *No Apologies Magazine*. "All Roads," *Amsterdam Quarterly*. "Glasgow Meeting," *Friends Journal*. Reprinted by permission of the author.

Dawn Potter: "Protestant Cemetery," *How the Crimes Happened* (CavanKerry Press). "Lullaby," *Boy Land (*Deerbrook Editions) and *Writer's Almanac*. "Nostalgia," *Boy Land* and *Writer's Almanac*. Reprinted by permission of the author.

Janice Miller Potter: "Psalm for Appalachia," *The Sow's Ear Poetry Review* and *Psalms in Time* (Finishing Line Press). "Our Boots Kept Wanting to Meld," *The Pittsburgh Quarterly*. Reprinted by permission of the author.

David Ray: "Doing Without," *Music of Time: Selected and New Poems* (Backwaters Press) and *Poetry 180*. "Having Too Much," *Music of Time: Selected and New Poems*. Reprinted by permission of the author.

Judy Ray: "Time on My Hands," *The National Catholic Reporter* and *Enlivened by the Mystery: Quakers and God* (Friends Bulletin Corporation). Reprinted by permission of the author.

Lauren Rusk: "Building Down," *Pictures in the Firestorm* (Plain View Press). Reprinted by permission of the author.

Sarah Sarai: "Something's Falling," *Threepenny Review*. "A Rhetorical Inquiry into the Moral Certitude of Cause and Effect," *Eleven Eleven*. "Remorse," *Terrain.org*. Reprinted by permission of the author.

Elizabeth Schultz: "Mrs. Noah Takes the Helm," *Flint Hills Review*. Reprinted by permission of the author.

Marian Kaplun Shapiro: "Quaker Meeting: Cambridge/Rangeley, Maine," *Players in the Dream, Dreamers in the Play* (Plain View Press). Reprinted by permission of the author.

Maryhelen Snyder: "Lamb of the Catalinas," *SLANT*. "Sun in an Empty Room," *Gettysburg Review*. "The Lesson," *Gettysburg Review*. Reprinted by permission of the author.

ABOUT THE EDITOR

Nick McRae is the author of *The Name Museum* (C&R Press)—winner of the De Novo Poetry Prize—as well as the chapbook *Mountain Redemption* (Black Lawrence Press). His poems appear in *Cincinnati Review*, *Hayden's Ferry Review*, *The Southern Review*, *Third Coast*, and elsewhere. He serves as an assistant editor and *Best of the Net* coordinator for Sundress Publications, associate editor for *32 Poems*, and is a member of the Sewanee Writers' Conference staff. A graduate of the M.F.A. program at Ohio State University, Nick is currently a Robert B. Toulouse Doctoral Fellow in English at the University of North Texas. He is a member of North Columbus Friends Meeting.

SUNDRESS PUBLICATIONS TITLES

THE OLD CITIES
MARCEL BROUWERS
$14.00 ISBN 0-9723224-9-3

ONE PERFECT BIRD
LETITIA TRENT
$14.95 ISBN 0-9723224-8-5

LIKE A FISH
DANIEL CROCKER
$14.95 ISBN 0-9723224-8-5

THE BONE FOLDERS
T.A. NOONAN
$14.95 ISBN 0-9723224-6-9

ESPECIALLY THE DEER
TYURINA ALLEN, MARY BETH MAGIN,
& JULIE RUBLE
$12.99 ISBN 0-9723224-0-X

CPSIA information can be obtained at www.ICGtesting.com
Printed in the USA
LVOW130701130613

338385LV00001B/33/P